WADSWORTH PHILOSOPHERS SERIES

'ON

RAWLS

A Liberal Theory of Justice and Justification

Robert B. Talisse
Hunter College, The City University of New York

Australia • Canada • Mexico • Singapore • Spain
United Kingdom • United States

For my parents: Pat and Bob Talisse

Printed in the United States of America
1 2 3 4 5 6 7 04 03 02 01 00

For permission to use material from this text, contact us:
Web: http://www.thomsonrights.com
Fax: 1-800-730-2215
Phone: 1-800-730-2214

For more information, contact:
Wadsworth/Thomson Learning, Inc.
10 Davis Drive
Belmont, CA 94002-3098
USA
http://www.wadsworth.com

ISBN: 0-534-58369-5

Table of Contents

Acknowledgments

D. Micah Hester of Mercer University once again has gone above and beyond the call of duty. Despite the fact that he was busy preparing a book of his own for publication, he managed to find the time to not only read and comment on each chapter of this text with eagerness and care but also to coach me in the task of formatting the manuscript according to Wadsworth's specifications. As with most of my work, this book owes much to Micah's generosity and wisdom. He again gets my deepest gratitude.

I have also benefited from the help of several friends. Drafts of these chapters were read by Robert Buckley, Danielle Iemola, Dave McCullough, Ed Taylor, and Robert Tempio. Due to their efforts, many errors, confusions, and lapses of clarity in both style and content have been corrected.

Informal discussions and arguments with colleagues have proved invaluable in my preparation of this study. In particular, I have benefited from conversation with Steven Cahn, Virginia Held, Dwight Goodyear, Angelo Juffras, Daniel Kolak, John O□Connor, John Peterman, Steven Ross, and Peter Simpson.

Finally, Joanne Billett deserves special notice. My work owes more to her unyielding support and encouragement than she realizes.

Abbreviations

I shall employ the following abbreviations for John Rawls's works in the parenthetical citations throughout the present work. Citations to the work of other philosophers will follow the standard author/date method. Consult the list of works cited at the end of this volume.

TJ =   *A Theory of Justice*. Revised Edition. Cambridge: Harvard University Press, 1999.

PL=   *Political Liberalism*. Paperback Edition. New York: Columbia University Press, 1996.

CP =   *John Rawls: Collected Papers*. Edited by Samuel Friedman. Cambridge: Harvard University Press, 1999.

Preface

This short book is an introduction to the political philosophy of John Rawls. Like the other titles in the Wadsworth Philosophers Series, it has been written with the needs of undergraduate students and general readers in mind. I have therefore assumed that my reader has had no prior exposure to the Western philosophical tradition. Accordingly, the technical jargon and style of argumentation which might otherwise be appropriate have been tamed; terms and concepts which are likely to be unfamiliar to general readers have been carefully explained. In short, I have endeavored to make this book accessible and helpful to those coming to Rawls and to political philosophy for the first time.

This is not to say that the following pages provide merely a textbook canvas of Rawls's main contentions. Readers in search of a Rawls study guide or a substitute for reading Rawls's own works will be disappointed by what they find in this text. Although I have adjusted the manner of presentation to suit my audience, this text retains a high degree of philosophical content. I have tried to place Rawls's thought within the context of the philosophical tradition from which it derives, and to cast Rawls's ideas within the context of the problems to which they are a response. Hence one can expect to be philosophically engaged throughout this book.

Whereas other great philosophers attempt to articulate a comprehensive system covering the full range of philosophical topics, Rawls's most important work is focused upon the formulation and defense of his theory of justice, which he calls "justice as fairness." As one would expect, Rawls's theory of justice is the topic of this book. Again, given my intended audience, I have for the most part focused the attention of this study on Rawls's two major works, *A Theory of Justice* (1971) and *Political Liberalism* (1993). Of course, Rawls has written in addition to these books several important and instructive articles and essays. I have cited these where necessary.

Although the main features of justice as fairness can be easily stated, the project of writing a brief but philosophically respectable introduction to Rawls presents a number of unique challenges. Foremost among these derive from the fact that Rawls's work has been so influential and stimulated so much comment. There presently exists a veritable mountain of secondary work relating to Rawls's ideas. Even a quick survey of this literature will demonstrate that all but the most elementary features of Rawls's view are the subjects of continuing scholarly controversy. Which of the leading styles of Rawls interpretation should be presented? To what degree should the main lines of criticism be represented? Is a philosophically responsible introduction to Rawls's political philosophy possible?

In thinking through such questions, I have come to the view that an effective introduction to Rawls must be also an introduction to the liberal tradition within modern and contemporary political philosophy. I have accordingly written this text to be a primer or prolegomenon to the study of Rawls rather than a comprehensive summation of or commentary on Rawls's political philosophy. To be sure, the basic contours of justice as fairness and political liberalism are faithfully presented and explained. However, I have elected to forego discussion of the more technical points of Rawls's theory, which, unsurprisingly, tend to be the target of the greatest dispute. Rather than getting mired in debates over the intricacies of some of Rawls's more obscure and unwieldy arguments, I have directed attention to the philosophical context of Rawls's work. For example, whereas considerable attention is given to the concept of liberalism as a kind of political theory, discussion of the details of Rawls's "maximin" argument, the many difficulties of which are familiar to any Rawls specialist, is absent. This is, I contend, the best way to accommodate a diverse audience in light of the aforementioned interpretative controversies. Recognizing that some readers will want to pursue further the specific details of Rawls's views, I have included throughout the text and in the endnotes citations to a variety of secondary material representing the most significant lines of criticism, commentary, and controversy. Hence, *On Rawls* is an introduction in the proper sense: it provides an initial encounter with Rawls on the basis of which one may pursue a deeper relationship.

1

Preliminary Considerations: John Rawls and Political Philosophy

John Rawls and His Influence

In 1995, Steve Pyke published a book of his photographs of influential living philosophers. Pyke's portrait of John Rawls is accompanied by the following remarks, Rawls's only autobiographical statement:

> From the beginning of my study of philosophy in my late teens I have been concerned with moral questions and the religious and philosophical basis on which they might be answered. Three years spent in the US Army in World War II led me to be concerned with political questions. Around 1950 I started to write a book on justice, which I eventually completed. (Rawls, in Pike 1995)

These humble remarks may at first seem fitting, for Rawls's life is in many ways conventional for a twentieth-century academic. John Rawls was born into a upper-middle class Baltimore family in 1921. He received his Bachelor of Arts degree from Princeton University in

1943, and joined the army. Rawls served as an infantryman in the Pacific during World War II. His tour of duty brought him to New Guinea, the Philippines, and Japan. Like many of his generation, Rawls witnessed first hand the dangers of nationalism and the evil of which persons caught in the grip of fanaticism are capable. Withdrawing from the military in 1946, Rawls returned to Princeton to pursue graduate work in philosophy, and was awarded a doctorate in 1950. He accepted a teaching appointment at Princeton and then won a Fullbright Fellowship at Oxford. Upon returning to the United States, Rawls accepted a position at Cornell University, where he taught until 1959. After a brief appointment at the Massachusetts Institute of Technology, Rawls moved to Harvard University in 1962. Today, he is the Conant University Professor Emeritus of Harvard.

There is, however, a certain irony in the modest tone of Rawls's autobiographical comments. The "book on justice" to which he so casually refers is his 1971 work, *A Theory of Justice*, a book that has sparked what may fairly be called a revolution in political philosophy. Within its pages, Rawls not only reinvented and reinvigorated the enterprise of political philosophy, but also proposed a fascinating and controversial philosophical theory called "justice as fairness."

The impact of Rawls's *A Theory of Justice* can hardly be overstated. In 1974, just three years after the publication of *A Theory of Justice*, Robert Nozick, himself a major philosopher, registered the following assessment of the significance Rawls's book:

> *A Theory of Justice* is a powerful, deep, subtle, wide-ranging, systematic work in political and moral philosophy which has not seen its like since the writings of John Stuart Mill, if then. It is a fountain of illuminating ideas, integrated together into a lovely whole. Political philosophers now must either work within Rawls's theory or explain why not. (Nozick, 183)

Nozick's estimation of Rawls's importance remains accurate today. The number of books and articles building upon, responding to, commenting on, and influenced by the ideas of John Rawls persistently increases, and it is almost impossible now to find a recent book on political theory which does not contain multiple references to Rawls's work. Indeed, philosopher Jonathan Wolff's claim that "Contemporary English-language political philosophy began in 1971, with the publication of John Rawls's *A Theory of Justice* . . . " (J. Wolff, 118) seems entirely appropriate.

It is a further indication of the gravity of Rawls's achievement that his work is recognized not only by professional philosophers;

Rawls is among the few contemporary philosophers whose work has exerted considerable influence over academic disciplines other than philosophy. Rawls's works are studied in departments of economics, political science, sociology, and in law schools throughout the world, and his ideas have helped to shape and develop these areas of inquiry. Even more remarkable is the fact that Rawls has gained the esteem of persons outside the academy. In 1999, President Bill Clinton awarded Rawls the National Humanities Medal. Conferring the award, Clinton said of Rawls:

> John Rawls is perhaps the greatest political philosopher of the twentieth century. In 1971, when Hillary and I were in law school, we were among the millions moved by a remarkable book he wrote, *A Theory of Justice*, that placed our rights to liberty and justice upon a strong and brilliant new foundation of reason. Almost singlehandedly, John Rawls revived the disciplines of political and ethical philosophy. . . . . he has helped a whole generation of learned Americans revive their faith in democracy itself. (U. S. President, 1852)

In light of these accolades, it is safe to conclude with philosopher Thomas Nagel that John Rawls is "the most important political philosopher of the twentieth century" (Nagel 1999, 36).

However, that Rawls is widely believed to be an important political philosopher should not suggest that his views are generally accepted as true. In fact, Rawls is one of today's most controversial political thinkers, and his theory of justice as fairness is the subject of continuing and often heated debate. In the estimation of the philosopher and legal theorist Michael Sandel, one of Rawls's most trenchant critics, *A Theory of Justice* "provoked not one debate, but three" (Sandel 1998, 184). This is a conservative estimate; Rawls's work has sparked debates in fields as diverse as rational choice theory, international politics, and social psychology. Rawls has been criticized for his method, his arguments, his premises, and his conclusions. Some have criticized Rawls for maintaining moral "subjectivism" (Hare 1973, 82), the view according to which there are no objective moral truths, whereas others have attacked him for his alleged "universalism" (Walzer, 5) the view that there are universal truths about social justice that can be applied to any society. He has been reproached by political radicals for being too conservative in his recommendations for economic redistribution and social change (Miller, 208ff.), and by political conservatives for being too radical on economic justice and governmental interference (Nozick, 183ff.). Some have charged that

Rawls's conception of justice is too narrow, and that his political theory is hence unable to address important social issues such as those concerning the political status of women (Baier; Held, 169-171) and children (Brennan and Noggle); others have maintained that justice as fairness is in fact unfair to persons holding certain religious beliefs (Sandel 1998, 210-218; Wenar; Quinn) or non-individualistic conceptions of the good life (Nagel 1973, 8-10).[1] Some critics have even argued that justice as fairness implies no definite political policies at all, and hence is a useless, academic abstraction (R. Wolff, 195; Michelman, 321f.; Barber 1975, 310).[2]

What's the big idea? What is "justice as fairness," and why has it stirred so much controversy? Why has Rawls, a theorist who almost nobody completely agrees with, been so influential? These questions will be answered in the course of this book. Before we can address Rawls's work in its own terms, however, we must first consider a few points regarding political philosophy and its history. Although Rawls is an original thinker, his theory fits neatly into a particular tradition of political philosophy; consequently, his work is best understood against the background of this tradition.

Political Philosophy: Classical and Modern

With the possible exception of the flattering principle that begins his *Metaphysics*, "All humans by nature desire knowledge," the ancient Greek philosopher Aristotle (384-322 B.C.E.) is most famous for the claim, made in his *Politics*, that "A human being is by nature a political animal" (Aristotle 1997, 1253a3).[3] This sentence is probably more often asserted than understood; once its meaning is made clear, it should seem obviously false to you. Aristotle's claim is likely to seem false because your own political thinking, even at the most basic, commonsense levels, is informed by and cast in terms of a distinctive approach to politics that differs significantly from Aristotle's approach. In the present section, we shall contrast Aristotle's understanding of political philosophy with a modern and familiar alternative known as *liberalism*. John Rawls's theory of justice as fairness is a liberal theory; hence a preliminary sketch of liberalism will prepare us for a more detailed examination of Rawls's work.

The Classical View of Politics: Aristotle's Theory

What did Aristotle mean when he claimed that we are by nature political? Aristotle's political philosophy is formulated in terms of his more general philosophical orientation, which we shall call *teleological naturalism*. This is, I admit, a clumsy name, however, its meaning is easily grasped with a little analysis. *'Telos'* is the Greek word for 'aim' or 'goal'. To use one of Aristotle's own examples, the bull's-eye of a target is the *telos* of the archer, it is that at which he aims, it is his goal; we might say further that hitting the bull's-eye is the *purpose* of the archer. Accordingly, an explanation that is *teleological* is one that explains an action or event in terms of the purpose at which it is aimed. So, if I were to ask you, *Why are you reading this sentence?*, and if you were to respond, *Because I want to understand the philosophy of John Rawls*, you would have offered a teleological explanation of your present action, you would have explained what you are doing in terms of what you aim to accomplish by means of your action.

What makes Aristotle's view a teleological *naturalism* is that he maintains that every naturally existing thing has a *telos,* a purpose, built in to it by nature. To use a common example, acorns by nature aim to become oak trees, and hence to make more acorns. Thus we may say that *what it is to be* an acorn is to be something that by nature strives to become an oak. In this way, the acorn is *defined* in terms of its purpose, its goal. Therefore, the oak is *prior* to the acorn in the order of explanation; that is, in order to understand what an acorn is, one must first understand what an oak is.

But we must not understand a *telos* as simply an "end" or "aim"; the idea of a *telos* as a natural purpose has a moral dimension as well. Aristotle's *Nicomachean Ethics* begins with the identification of the *telos* of a thing with the "good" of that thing (Aristotle 1962, 1094a1-5). To see this, consider that as the acorn is by nature something that aims to be an oak, it is *in itself* necessarily incomplete and unfulfilled. In becoming an oak, the acorn "realizes" or "completes" itself, it fulfills its natural purpose. Since it is the very nature of an acorn to become an oak tree, the "perfected" acorn is the oak. Therefore what is "good" for the acorn is that which assists it in attaining its *telos*. In this sense, a *telos* is a "perfection," and that which directs a thing to its perfection is good for that thing.

Now that we understand Aristotle's teleological naturalism, we must ask, What has it to do with politics? Aristotle maintains that as human beings are naturally existing things, we too have a natural *telos,*

7

which Aristotle calls *eudaimonia*, "happiness" or "well-being" (Aristotle 1962, 1095a20). All of our actions ultimately aim at happiness, and the "complete" and best human life is the one in which happiness is attained. Therefore what is "good" for a human is that which assists in realizing happiness.

Although happiness is the natural purpose of a human being, persons hold different views about what happiness is. Some say that the happy life is the life of acquiring wealth or honor; others say it is the life of experiencing pleasure (Aristotle 1962, 1095a22). According to Aristotle, such views about what constitutes the happy life are wrong. Someone who believes that the best life is the one that contains the most pleasure is mistaken; similarly, someone who devotes his life to acquiring wealth is living badly. In his *Nicomachean Ethics*, Aristotle argues that the happy life is one of developing and exercising one's rational abilities (Aristotle 1962, 1098a12-15). We cannot here examine Aristotle's view in full; our point is that whereas each of us by nature seeks to be happy and live well, one may be mistaken about what happiness consists in and hence pursue the wrong things in life.

If one is truly to live well, then, one needs to acquire the correct conception of happiness. Aristotle maintains that persons derive their conception of happiness from "the lives which they lead" (Aristotle 1962, 1095b15). That is, one's conception of what happiness consists in is primarily a function of one's upbringing, one's education, and one's culture; a person "must receive a good upbringing and discipline in order to be good" (Aristotle 1962, 1180a15). According to Aristotle, then, one cannot live a good life by oneself; happiness requires the effort of other people, particularly those people who will provide the requisite upbringing, education, and discipline. The tasks associated with upbringing and education are performed and managed by social associations such as the family, the neighborhood, and the state.[4] Therefore, human beings must live socially if they are to attain happiness; without properly organized social associations, happiness is impossible.

Since good families, neighborhoods, and states are necessary for happiness, and since happiness is the natural aim of human beings, families, neighborhoods, and states are also naturally existing things; that which is necessary for the achievement of the *telos* of a natural thing itself exists by nature. Aristotle argues that, of the kinds of social association, the state is most important (Aristotle 1997, 1252a1-5). This is because the family and the neighborhood can exist only as *parts* of a state. Just as one cannot understand an acorn except in terms of an oak tree, one cannot understand the family and the neighborhood except in

8

terms of the state to which they belong. Hence, on Aristotle's view, the state is the primary mode of social association.

As it exists by nature, the state also has a natural purpose, and that is the moral perfection of its citizens. It is the proper function of the state to assist humans in living good lives by instituting legislation which forces persons to behave rightly from the time they are very young. Hence according to Aristotle, the state "exists for the sake of living well" (Aristotle 1997, 1252b27); its primary job is that of establishing and enforcing laws which reflect the correct view of happiness. That is, the state must make people morally good.

Now we can understand what Aristotle's famous remark means. Since it is the purpose of a human being to be happy, and since happiness can be achieved only within a good state, a human being is *by nature* political in that he is *by nature* a citizen, a member of a state. Hence we may say that what it is to be a human being is to be a citizen; citizenship is in part what *defines* a human being. Indeed, Aristotle claims that a being who by nature can live without a state is *ipso facto* not a human being, but "either a beast or a god" (Aristotle 1997, 1253a27).

There are four implications of Aristotle's claim that human beings are naturally political which are especially important for our present purposes. First, if what it is to be human is to be a member of a state, then the state is in a sense prior to the individual person (Aristotle 1997, 1253a18). Although each of us is born into a pre-existing state, the priority that Aristotle means is not primarily temporal. According to Aristotle, the state is morally prior to the individual; that is, on Aristotle's view, the good of the state takes precedence over the good of the individual. Aristotle writes:

> Even if the good is the same for the individual and the state,
> the good of the state clearly is the greater and more perfect
> thing to attain and to safeguard. The attainment of the good for
> one man is, to be sure, a source of satisfaction yet to secure it
> for a nation and for states is nobler and more divine. (Aristotle
> 1962, 1094b6-10)

As the good state is necessary for the development of good citizens, the good of the state is morally more important than the good of any particular citizen.

Second, if happiness is the natural *telos* of human beings, and if happiness can be attained only within the right kind of state, it follows that those humans living in a state which does not promote the correct way of life are necessarily unhappy and living unnatural and depraved

9

lives. As the state exists for the purpose of living well, a state which promotes the wrong view of happiness, or which promotes no particular view of happiness at all, is not performing its proper function. Accordingly, such states are corrupt and unjust.

Third, if happiness is the *telos* of human beings, and if happiness consists in the development and exercise of one's rational abilities, then persons lacking in rational ability will not be fully human. Hence Aristotle notoriously argues that some human beings are by nature "deficient." Aristotle recognizes two kinds of human beings who are by nature "corrupt" and "defective": women and what he calls "natural slaves" (Aristotle 1997, 1254a13). Women and natural slaves are, according to Aristotle, human beings who, for various reasons, are by nature not fully rational.[5] They are therefore by nature subordinate to rational men who are by nature their rulers. Moreover, because they are incapable of developing their rational abilities, women and natural slaves are unfit for citizenship; accordingly, a state which extends full citizenship to those who by nature are not full citizens is corrupt.

Finally, if the proper aim of the state is the moral perfection of its citizens, and if the citizens can be improved only through the right kind of education and laws, then the good state is the one with correct laws and educational institutions. However, proper laws and institutions can be established and maintained only by those who know what is morally correct. Hence the best state is one in which the morally best men have control. Aristotle thus endorses a political arrangement in which the best men rule over the others. Accordingly, Aristotle views democracy as a "corrupt" kind of state (Aristotle 1997, 1279a22-1279b4).

It is important to note that Aristotle's view does not simply present a series of suggestions for political policy; it is representative of a specific approach to political philosophy, a certain conception of what political philosophy is. We may call the general approach to political philosophy of which Aristotle's view is an example the "classical" approach. According to the classical approach, the enterprise of political philosophy is primarily concerned with the highest good, and its main objective is that of identifying the political arrangement most conducive to the realization of the best way of life for humans.[6]

The classical approach to politics enjoyed considerable influence throughout history; however, the advent of modern science brought with it the abandonment of Aristotle's teleological naturalism. We no longer believe that nature installs *purposes* into things; nor do we accept teleological explanations of natural events. With the metaphysical presuppositions of the classical view displaced, there arose a new way of thinking about politics.[7] Accordingly, contemporary political philosophy, and much of our own everyday political thinking, is conducted in terms of assumptions which are altogether different from those underlying the classical approach.

The Modern View of Politics: Liberalism

It is not uncommon today to hear the term "liberalism" used to characterize the platform of the Democratic party in the United States. In popular discourse, "liberalism" is contrasted with "conservatism," a term which in turn is used to characterize the political platform of the Republican party in the United States. However, "liberalism," as it is used in political philosophy, and as we shall use it in this study, has a different meaning. In political philosophy, "liberalism" is the name of a distinctively modern approach to political theory rather than the platform of a political party.[8]

The principal features of the liberal approach are well expressed by Thomas Jefferson in the *Declaration of Independence*:

> We hold these truths to be self-evident, that all men are created equal, that they are endowed by their Creator with certain unalienable Rights, that among these are Life, Liberty, and the pursuit of Happiness. That to secure these rights, Governments are instituted among Men, deriving their just powers from the consent of the governed, That whenever a Form of Government becomes destructive of these ends, it is the Right of the People to alter or to abolish it, and to institute a new Government, laying its foundations on such principles and organizing powers in such form, as to them shall seem most likely to effect their Safety and Happiness. (Jefferson, 601)

More recently, Martha Nussbaum has offered the following statement:

> Liberalism holds that the flourishing of human beings taken one by one is both analytically and normatively prior to the flourishing of the state or the nation or the religious group; analytically, because such unities do not really efface the separate reality of individual lives; normatively because the recognition of that separateness is held to be a fundamental fact for ethics, which should recognize each separate entity as an end and not as a means to the ends of others. (Nussbaum, 62)

11

Allen Buchanan has proposed a similar characterization:

> The liberal political thesis, as I define it, is the thesis that the state should enforce certain basic civil and individual rights and liberties-- roughly speaking, those which are found in the U. S. Constitution's Bill of Rights . . . . These rights include rights to freedom of religion, expression, thought, and association, the right of political participation, and the right of due process. This first thesis is closely related to, and may be argued to imply another thesis that is also associated with liberalism, namely that the proper role of the state is to protect basic individual liberties, not to make its citizens virtuous or to impose upon them any particular or substantive conception of the good life. The connection between these theses should be clear: if the state enforces the basic civil and political liberties, it will leave individuals free, within broad limits, to pursue their own conceptions of the good and will preclude itself from imposing upon them any one particular conception of the good or of virtue. (Buchanan 1989, 854)

These three statements express the basics of the liberal view of politics.[9] In contrast to Aristotle, liberals begin from the premise that humans are by nature *apolitical*; individuals are not, as Aristotle would have it, essentially *citizens*, but rather free, equal, and independent agents in pursuit of the satisfaction of their own interests. In virtue of their natural freedom and equality, individuals are possessed of rights that establish, among other things, a realm of individual action that is properly free from governmental and social interference. Individual rights place *constraints* upon what a state, or any social group, can do to an individual. Liberals maintain that an individual's liberty consists in his ability to exercise his natural rights without obstruction or interference from others.[10]

Furthermore, on the liberal view, states do not exist *by nature*, as Aristotle held, but rather are human artifacts. That is, states exist because individuals have created them, and where states do exist their chief function is the protection of individuals and their natural rights. The state protects its citizens by enforcing laws that apply equally to everybody (including the agents of the state), allowing for the greatest degree of individual freedom consistent with equal freedom for all. Consequently, the state's role is not that of moral tutor, as Aristotle maintained, but those of night watchman and umpire; the state's job is to maintain order, to protect the lives and property of citizens, to fairly resolve disputes, and to punish those who violate the rights of others.

12

As its job is primarily protective and not formative, the liberal state is not concerned with the moral perfection of its citizens; in fact, liberals are skeptical of the Aristotelian idea that there is but a single way to live a good life. As Rawls says, "individuals find their good in different ways, and many things may be good for one person that would not be good for another" (*TJ*, 393). Thus citizens are to be left on their own to discover what is valuable and worthy of pursuit in life, to "determine their own good" (*TJ*, 393). This freedom to pursue what one judges to be good is on the liberal view perhaps the most basic freedom; as the nineteenth century philosopher, John Stuart Mill contends, "The only freedom which deserves the name is that of pursuing our own good in our own way" (Mill, 17). Of course, an individual's pursuit of his own good is subject to a familiar constraint: he must not impede or obstruct others who are pursuing their own goods. Once my pursuit of what I have judged to be good interferes with or obstructs your pursuit of your own chosen ends, the state may get involved and restrain me. Accordingly, so long as the individual does not interfere with anyone else, he "may pursue his own happiness in the manner that seems best to him" (Kant, 74).

Accordingly, any state that seeks to promote any particular moral vision or conception of the good life upon its citizens is oppressive and therefore unjust; according to the liberal, disagreement about what constitutes the best life is the mark of a free society (*PL*, 37). In the liberal state, then, government policy and decision must be, in the words of legal theorist Ronald Dworkin, "so far as possible independent of any particular conception of the good life, or of what gives value to life" (Dworkin 1978, 127).[11] Consequently, a liberal society accepts that citizens will elect to pursue different kinds of lives: they will worship different gods or no gods at all, they will value different things, they will devote their individual lives to different projects. That is, liberal citizens and states must be *tolerant* of different ways of life. Indeed, as differences of opinion with regard to the good life are the necessary outcome of freedom, such differences among citizens are to be celebrated as "not an evil, but a good" (Mill, 62). Hence we today hear much talk of the good of "diversity."

Moreover, on the liberal view, the individual and his good is prior to the good of the state and any other social group. Hence the good of the individual cannot be sacrificed for the good of the state; Rawls writes, "Each person possesses an inviolability founded on justice that even the welfare of society as a whole cannot override" (*TJ*, 3). In contrast with the Aristotelian view, liberals hold that the state exists for the purpose of *serving* the ends of its citizens. Accordingly, the state is

13

answerable to those it governs. It must win the *consent* of its citizens; otherwise, as Jefferson notes above, it may be rightfully abolished.

Even critics of liberalism acknowledge that it "offers a powerful liberating vision" (Sandel 1996, 12). The liberal image of free, equal, and independent individuals pursuing their own conceptions of the good life and allowing others to pursue theirs is especially well-suited to democratic political arrangements. Insofar as the liberal state requires the consent of the free and equal persons it governs, it must devise and maintain institutions and procedures by which citizens can regularly voice their preferences as regards political policy. Accordingly, democracy, a system of government in which each citizens has an equal say in drafting the policies by which they all shall be governed, is the natural companion to a liberal politics.

The Classical and Modern Views Contrasted

We have now sketched two competing political visions. We may say that whereas classical thinkers such as Aristotle promoted a view according to which the ultimate concern of the state is the highest human good and the moral perfection of individual persons, liberals offer an alternative view according to which the main focus of political association is the freedom of individuals to decide questions of the highest humans good for themselves, and to pursue the kind of life they judge most worthy. To draw the contrast in a slightly different way, classical political philosophy is focused primarily on the state and its moral function whereas the liberal view is focused upon the individual and his freedom. Hence, classical political philosophers such as Aristotle are concerned with the question, Within what kind of state is the good life achieved? The classical view thereby assumes the *necessity* of the state. By contrast, Robert Nozick writes,

> Individuals have rights, and there are things no person or group may do to them (without violating their rights). So strong and far-reaching are these rights that they raise the question of what, if anything, the state and its officials may do. How much room do individual rights leave for the state? (Nozick, ix)

According to Nozick, "The fundamental question of political philosophy, one that precedes questions about how the state should be organized, is whether there should be a state at all" (Nozick, 4).[12]

Liberalism and Contemporary Politics

The liberal conception of political theory should sound familiar to you. As was perhaps suggested by my use of the Jefferson quote above, the political philosophy of liberalism played a prominent role in the founding of the United States. Today it sets the vocabulary with which we discuss political issues. We may say then that liberalism provides the "framework" within which our contemporary political discourse is conducted.

Indeed, today's most contentious social and political issues-- abortion, affirmative action, gun control, capital punishment, drug prohibition, for example-- are debated in terms of individual rights and competing interests, and thus presume the liberal framework. So whereas we often hear gun control advocates argue that the availability of guns is directly related to violence and the loss of innocent lives, we rarely, if ever, hear someone arguing for gun control legislation on the grounds that gun ownership interferes with attaining happiness. Similarly, those who advocate the legalization of certain drugs appeal to the rights of individuals to decide for themselves whether to use drugs; rarely is it argued that drug use should be legal because it is a necessary component of the good life.

An Example: Pornography

By way of further illustration, let us examine briefly the current and perhaps familiar policy dispute concerning pornography. Our aim here is not to decide the policy questions, but rather to examine *how* the issue is framed in current political discussions.

The contemporary debate over pornography is conducted almost exclusively within the liberal framework: the issue of whether pornographic material should be banned is framed in terms of the competing rights involved. Persons who oppose a legal ban on pornographic material cite the First Amendment of the U.S. Constitution which disallows the abridgement of free speech. However, some argue that pornography is causally linked to acts of violence against women and to the existence of socially pervasive attitudes about women and sexuality which promote practices that are unfair to women; pornography, it is alleged, therefore constitutes a violation of the civil rights of women and should thus be legally prohibited.

15

These modes of political analysis are evident in the round of debates concerning a controversial amendment proposed to the Minneapolis Civil Rights Ordinance in 1983—later proposed in 1984 to the City Council of Indianapolis—claiming that pornography "is a form of discrimination on the basis of sex" and thus should be subject to extensive legal regulation.[13] In support of the ordinance, legal theorist Catherine MacKinnon argues,

> The harm of pornography, broadly speaking, is the harm of the civil inequality of the sexes made invisible as harm because it has become accepted as the sex difference. (MacKinnon, 63)

Supporting MacKinnon's position, philosopher Rae Langton writes,

> Women are apparently disadvantaged by the permissive policy [regarding pornography] . . . . it is probably that the existence of such pornography reinforces and perpetuates attitudes and beliefs that undermine the well-being of women and undermine sexual equality; it probably contributes, for example, to an environment in which sexual abuse is more likely to occur. (Langton, 106-107)

Ronald Dworkin, who maintains that the proposed Indianapolis ordinance is unconstitutional, argues,

> Lawyers who defend the Indianapolis ordinance argue that society does have a further justification for outlawing pornography: that it causes great harm as well as offence to women. But their arguments mix together claims about different kinds of harm, and it is necessary to distinguish these. They argue, first, that some forms of pornography significantly increase the danger that women will be raped or physically assaulted. If that were true, and the danger were clear and present, then it would indeed justify censorship of those forms . . . . In fact, however, though there is some evidence that exposure to pornography weakens people's critical attitudes towards sexual violence, there is no persuasive evidence that it causes more actual incidents of assault. (Dworkin 1993, 117)

In each case, one finds that the relevant consideration in determining the status of a prohibition on pornography is the degree to which it harms women. Those who support anti-pornography laws argue that pornography does harm women in a way sufficient to warrant legal prohibition. Those who reject anti-pornography legislation deny that pornography harms sufficiently to require special action.

16

This is not to say, however, that those who support the rights of pornographers and consumers of pornographic material believe that pornography is morally unproblematic. On a liberal analysis, the question of the moral value of pornography is irrelevant. For the liberal, the issue turns not upon the moral effects of exposure to pornography on the characters of those who consume it, or the morality of participation in the industry which produces pornography; the liberal's commitment to moral neutrality requires that policies are, insofar as possible, neutral with regard to questions of the good. The determining consideration is simply whether the production and distribution of pornography violates anyone's rights.

Hence in opposing the ordinance Ronald Dworkin did not argue that pornography is good; in fact, he may even believe that pornography is morally bad. In advocating the rights of pornographers and consumers of pornography, Dworkin did not register personal moral approval of pornography. Central to the liberal framework is the distinction between approving of a practice and recognizing an individual's right to engage in it. As the liberal framework divorces politics from morality, the liberal can consistently argue against legislation banning that which he finds morally disagreeable. Michael Sandel has articulated the point nicely:

> Liberals often take pride in defending what they oppose—pornography, for example, or unpopular views. They say the state should not impose a preferred way of life, but should leave its citizens as free as possible to choose their own values and ends, consistent with a similar liberty for others. This commitment to freedom of choice requires liberals constantly to distinguish between permission and praise, between allowing a practice and endorsing it. It is one thing to allow pornography, they argue, something else to affirm it. (Sandel 1984a, 1)

A Final Point about Liberalism

A final point about liberalism is in order before moving on. We noted above that the term "liberalism" as it is used in political philosophy differs from the sense it is given in popular political discussion. In popular discussion, you will recall, the "liberal" is contrasted with the "conservative." However, we now can see that both

17

"liberals" and "conservatives" are liberals in the philosophical sense of the term. Debates in the United States between Democrats and Republicans are *not* debates about liberalism in the philosophical sense; both parties accept the basic premises of liberalism, namely, that it is the state's job to protect the freedom of its citizens. How this liberal function is best performed is where the parties differ.

Generally speaking, Democrats maintain that part of what it is to protect the rights and liberties of individuals is to help maintain the social and economic conditions necessary for the effective exercise of individual rights. Democrats hence tend to support government programs designed to redistribute social goods such as wealth, education, and healthcare. Republicans, by contrast, tend to believe that the free market is a sufficient means to social justice. Republicans hence support policies that promote competition among providers of goods; in this sense, they maintain that the state should intervene as little as possible in distributive issues.

Of course, the positions of Republicans and Democrats do not exhaust the range of liberal politics; there are other options. Socialists, for example, tend to favor more complete forms of state control of social goods; some even advocate state ownership of the means by which social goods are produced. Libertarians, on the other hand, maintain a non-interventionism that is more extreme than that of the Republicans. One prominent libertarian advocates a state restricted to "the narrow functions of protection against force, theft, fraud, enforcement of contracts, and so on" (Nozick, ix); on the libertarian view, everything should be handled by the private sector and the free market.[14]

The Idea of a Theory of Justice

The Subject and Task of a Theory of Justice

There is hence a wide array of political options within the framework of liberalism. Which of these is best? How extensive should government intervention be? To what degree should wealth be redistributed? What principles should guide government policies and decisions in a liberal society? In asking such questions, we have opened the issue of justice. According to Rawls, "Justice is the first virtue of social institutions, as truth is of systems of thought" (*TJ*, 3). That is, as a system of thought must be rejected if it is untrue, justice is that characteristic of a social system without which the society would be unacceptable. Of course, the term "justice" is used in many different ways; for example, we often hear the word "just" used to describe entities as diverse as governments, laws, court decisions, and individual actions. However, Rawls is concerned primarily with *social* justice, the justice of what he calls the "basic structure" of a society. Rawls writes:

> For us, the primary subject of justice is the basic structure of society, or more exactly, the way in which the major social institutions distribute fundamental rights and duties and determine the division of advantages from social cooperation.[15] (*TJ*, 6)

In his later work, Rawls further explains the meaning of the "basic structure" as follows:

> By the basic structure I mean a society's main political, social, and economic institutions, and how they fit together into one unified system of social cooperation from one generation to the next.[16] (*PL*, 11)

The primary question of justice is, on Rawls's view, the question of how the "main political, social, and economic institutions" of a society should be organized.

Given this, we can say that a *conception of justice* is the collection of principles by which a society distributes rights, social goods, duties, and responsibilities. Every social group, insofar as it exhibits any stable scheme of cohesion and cooperation at all, will realize some conception of justice; that is, every assembly of persons which can properly be called a "social group" will exhibit implicit principles of organization which determine the roles, rules, and responsibilities of the individuals of which it is comprised. It is the project of a *theory of justice* to provide a systematic account of these principles and the logical relations between them which can serve as a reliable guide to further action and policy.

Accordingly, there are many conceptions of justice and many theories of justice. Moreover, there are several *liberal* conceptions of justice and several *liberal* theories of justice. A theory of justice is liberal if it specifies and systematizes a liberal conception of justice. A conception of justice is liberal if it is premised upon the basic philosophical claims of liberalism identified above. That is, a liberal conception of justice begins from the ideas that the rights of free and equal individuals are primary, that states exist because individuals choose to create and sustain them, and that the state's function is that of protecting its citizens and their rights. Hence we might say that

19

liberalism does not resolve the question of justice, rather it frames it; liberalism sets the task for a theory of justice. A successful liberal theory of justice will affirm and systematize the basic philosophical commitments of liberalism in a way which renders them logically coherent and which provides guidance in deciding social policy.

The Role of "Considered Judgments"

Rawls's objective in *A Theory of Justice* is to provide a liberal theory of justice that is superior to alternate liberal theories. What does it mean for one theory of justice to be superior to another? How can this superiority be shown? Unlike many traditional philosophers who thought that opposing moral or political theories were to be evaluated according to how well they correspond to the "facts" about human nature, Rawls adopts what may be called a "coherentist" view of justification.[17] On Rawls's view, competing theories of justice are to be evaluated according to how well they comport with what he calls our "considered judgments" about social justice (*TJ*, 40-46). By "considered judgments," Rawls means those moral evaluations that seem to us, upon reflection, especially sound and that are hence intuitively regarded as relatively fixed and basic facts with which any proposed theory of justice must comply. As Rawls explains:

> There are questions which we feel sure must be answered in a certain way. For example, we are confident that religious intolerance and racial discrimination are unjust. We think that we have examined these things with care and have reached what we believe is an impartial judgment not likely to be distorted by an excessive attention to our own interests. These convictions are provisional fixed points which we presume any conception of justice must fit. (*TJ*, 17-18; cf. *PL*, 8)

Picking up on Rawls's example of racial discrimination, we could imagine a theory of justice according to which the basic structure of society should be organized to grant social and economic advantages to persons according to race. Such a theory would strike us as intuitively unacceptable, for it fails to comply with one of our most firmly held moral convictions, namely, that racial discrimination is unjust. This failure to fit our considered judgment provides *prima facie* grounds for rejecting the proposed theory. We in fact hold several such judgments; our opposition to sexual discrimination and slavery provide further

20

examples, as do our commitments to religious liberty and freedom of expression.

Hence Rawls has proposed a way of evaluating competing theories of justice. At the very least, a theory of justice must "match our considered convictions of justice" (*TJ*, 17). Any theory according to which, for example, slavery or the suppression of religious views is permissible will be rejected. However, a good theory of justice will not amount to only a systematic catalogue of our intuitive judgments about justice; a theory of justice must also "provide guidance where guidance is needed" (*TJ*, 18). Whereas we are relatively certain that racial discrimination and religious intolerance are unjust, "we have much less assurance as to what is the correct distribution of wealth and authority" (*TJ*, 18). Therefore a theory of justice must also prescribe principles with which these matters may be dealt with. It is a further mark of a good theory of justice that these further principles comport well with our considered judgments; they must strike us as intuitively reasonable.

With these preliminary considerations in place, we turn directly to an exposition of *A Theory of Justice*.

Endnotes

[1] See the articles in Held, ed., and in George and Wolfe, eds.

[2] See Pogge for an attempt to derive specific political policies from Rawls's theory; see Crisp and Jamieson for a critique of Pogge's Rawls. For additional lines of general criticism, see Alejandro; Barry; Frohlich and Oppenheimer; Kymlicka 1989, Ch. 3; Kekes, Chs. 6 and 7; Sandel 1998; and the essays in Blocker and Smith, eds.

[3] Citations to the works of Aristotle will be keyed to the standard "Bekker numbering." So, line 1253a3 of Aristotle's *Politics* will be the same in every edition of Aristotle's works.

[4] Aristotle's words are *oikia* ("household"), *koma* ("village"), and *polis* ("city") (Aristotle 1997, 1252b9-35); "family," "neighborhood" and "state" are my own renderings.

[5] Aristotle claims that the slave lacks the "deliberative element" whereas the woman has it, but it does not control her actions (Aristotle 1997, 160a12).

[6] Aristotle calls politics the "most sovereign and most comprehensive master science" (Aristotle 1965, 1094a27).

[7] Some, however, do endorse a classical view of political theory; see, for example, MacIntyre, Sandel 1996; Beiner; and Simpson.

[8] Liberalism is "modern" in that it has its origin in the modern

period of the history of philosophy. Philosophy's modern period runs roughly from the 17th century to the present. In addition to Jefferson, who is cited below, the most influential historical expressions of liberalism can be found in the work of thinkers such as John Locke (1632-1704), Adam Smith (1723-1790), Immanuel Kant (1724-1804), and John Stuart Mill (1806-1873).

[9] See Ryan 1995 for a more complete exposition.

[10] That is, liberals hold what is known as a "negative" theory of freedom; on this see Isaiah Berlin's famous essay, "Two Concepts of Liberty" (Berlin 1958). For critical views, see Taylor, and Pettit 1997, Ch. 1.

[11] There are some liberal theorists who reject this. "Perfectionist" liberals, as they are sometimes called, hold that "it is the goal of all political action to enable individuals to pursue valid conceptions of the good and to discourage evil or empty ones" (Raz 1986, 133). See also Sher.

[12] Political scientist Benjamin Barber criticizes liberalism for its "anarchist disposition" (Barber 1984, 6-11); in a similar vein, sociologist Amitai Etzioni worries about liberalism's "self-centered, me-istic orientations" (Etzioni 1993, 24).

[13] The ordinance was drafted by Catherine MacKinnon and Andrea Dworkin in 1983, and is reprinted in the Appendix to Dwyer 1995. The ordinance was vetoed by the mayor of Minneapolis, and ruled unconstitutional by the district court of Indianapolis (a ruling upheld by the Supreme Court in 1986).

[14] According to Nozick, the scheme of taxation imposed upon citizens for purposes of funding social programs such as public education and healthcare is "on a par with forced labor" (Nozick, 169).

[15] Cf. "The primary subject of the principles of social justice is the basic structure of society, the arrangement of major social institutions into one scheme of cooperation" (*TJ*, 47).

[16] In Rawls's later work, "basic structure" becomes a somewhat technical term. See especially "The Basic Structure as Subject" (*PL*, Lecture VII).

[17] "A conception of justice cannot be deduced from self-evident premises or conditions on principles; instead, its justification is a matter of the mutual support of many considerations, of everything fitting together into one coherent view" (*TJ*, 19); see also *TJ* 506-514, and Rawls's 1951 paper, "Outline of a Decision Procedure for Ethics" (*CP*, 1-19). Helpful discussions can be found in Lyons; Hare 1973; Dworkin 1973, 27-37; and Daniels 1996.

22

2
Justice as Fairness

Towards a New Theory of Liberal Justice

We begin with one of Rawls's own statements concerning the nature of a conception of justice:

> Let us assume . . . that a society is a more or less self-sufficient association of persons who in their relations to one another recognize certain rules of conduct as binding and who for the most part act in accordance with them. Suppose further that these rules specify a system of cooperation designed to advance the good of those taking part in it. Then, although a society is a cooperative venture for mutual advantage, it is typically marked by a conflict as well as by an identity of interests. There is an identity of interests since social cooperation makes possible a better life for all than any would have if each were to live solely by his own efforts. There is a conflict of interests since persons are not indifferent as to how the greater benefits produced by their collaboration are distributed, for in order to pursue their ends they each prefer a larger to a lesser share. A set of principles is required for choosing among the various social arrangements which determine this division of advantages and for underwriting an agreement on the proper distributive shares. These principles

23

are the principles of social justice: they provide a way of
assigning rights and duties in the basic institutions of society
and they define the appropriate distribution of the benefits and
burdens of social cooperation.[1] (*TJ*, 4)

In this quote, we see Rawls laying out the basic presumptions of the
liberal view of politics: individuals enter into social arrangements for
the purpose of attaining benefits unavailable to them singularly;
accordingly, a society is a "cooperative venture" aimed at the "mutual
advantage" of the individuals that comprise it. As individuals do not
share a common good in the Aristotelian sense, but pursue interests
which at least sometimes conflict, there is a need for a system of rules
and institutions which establish "rights and duties" and distribute the
"benefits and burdens" of social living. As you will recall from the
previous chapter, this system of rules and institutions is what Rawls
calls the "basic structure" of society, and the principles upon which the
basic structure of a given society is based constitute its conception of
justice. A theory of justice is a philosophical articulation and
systematization of a conception of justice. The evaluation, criticism,
and defense of theories of justice is the main task of political
philosophy.

Let us adopt the stance of the political philosopher and ask
ourselves, What is the best conception of justice? According to Rawls,
we are in part asking, Which conception of justice "best approximates
our considered judgments of justice" (*TJ*, xviii)? One popular and
intuitively appealing answer to this question is the conception of justice
known as *utilitarianism*. Before examining Rawls's own theory, then,
we shall have a look at utilitarianism and Rawls's criticisms of it.

Rawls Versus Utilitarianism

At the time Rawls wrote *A Theory of Justice*, the dominant liberal
theory of justice was utilitarianism. Although there are several varieties
of utilitarianism, the main idea of the theory is well stated by Rawls:

The main idea [of utilitarianism] is that society is rightly
ordered, and therefore just, when its major institutions are
arranged so as to achieve the greatest net balance of
satisfaction summed over all the individuals belonging to it.
(*TJ*, 20)

More specifically, utilitarianism is a theory based upon a prior theory
of value known as *hedonism*. Hedonism is the view which holds that

"pleasure" (or "satisfaction" or "utility") is the only thing of *intrinsic* value.[2] To say that only satisfaction is *intrinsically* valuable is to say that it is the only thing which is good for its own sake; all other goods—such as, for example, health, friendship, wealth, or honesty—are *instrumentally* valuable, valuable only insofar as they produce or lead to satisfaction. As satisfaction is the only thing of intrinsic value, satisfaction is the only thing that is intrinsically good.

With hedonism in place, the utilitarian next takes the intuitive step of asserting that those actions are morally right that maximize what is intrinsically good. Further, as satisfaction is good, and dissatisfaction bad, no matter who is experiencing it, actions are morally right insofar as they maximize satisfaction (and minimize dissatisfaction) for *the greatest number of persons possible*. Hence utilitarianism has a "deep intuitive appeal": it identifies what is intrinsically good, and then defines morally right action as that which maximizes this good (*TJ*, 21).

When applied to an entire society as a conception of justice, utilitarianism maintains that social and political institutions, principles, and policies are morally proper, and hence just, in the degree to which they tend to maximize average utility (and minimize average disutility) for the entire society. Rawls claims that this idea is also appealing:

> . . . each man in realizing his own interests is certainly free to balance his own losses against his own gains. We may impose a sacrifice on ourselves now for the sake of a greater advantage later. A person quite properly acts, at least when others are not affected, to achieve his own greatest good, to advance his rational ends as far as possible. Now why should not a society act on precisely that same principle applied to the group and therefore regard that which is rational for one man as right for an association of men? . . . . And so by these reflections one reaches the principle of utility in a natural way: a society is properly arranged when its institutions maximize the net balance of satisfaction.[3] (*TJ*, 21)

Indeed, utilitarianism again seems to embody common sense. More good in the world is better than less good; therefore, as morally right action consists in producing as much good as one's circumstances permit, the just society is the one in which the basic structure is designed to maximize average good across its entire population.

It is important to note that utilitarians derive their conception of political justice from their moral theory, and hence ultimately from their hedonistic theory of value. Thus we may say that, for the utilitarian, the good is *prior* to the right (*TJ*, 21-22).[4] Accordingly, the utilitarian advocates those political arrangements which tend to maximize aggregate utility, whatever they may be. It has been the task of liberal utilitarians to show that liberal political arrangements and institutions *in fact* maximize the general good of society.[5] The utilitarian hence understands political "rights" to be especially reliable means for maximizing general satisfaction. In his 1861 book, *Utilitarianism*, John Stuart Mill writes,

> To have a right, then, is, I conceive, to have something which society ought to defend me in the possession of. If the objector goes on to ask why it ought, I can give him no other reason than general utility. (Mill 1991, 189)

Hence if we were to ask a utilitarian why society should recognize basic liberal rights, such as rights to free speech, assembly, and religious practice, the utilitarian would respond that a society which acknowledges such rights tends to generate more overall satisfaction among its citizens than any alternative form of society.

This reply may seem at first thoroughly reasonable. However, the utilitarian defense of liberal policies and liberal political rights raises significant difficulties. As utilitarians endorse liberal basic rights as *means* to the production of what they conceive as good, their commitment to those rights is ultimately *contingent* upon existing social conditions. Were we to pose circumstances under which average utility across society would be maximized if some individual's or small group of individuals' basic rights were violated, the utilitarian would have to endorse policies designed to violate those rights. We could, for example, imagine a vast majority that is especially opposed to the views of a small religious group. If it could be shown that the suppression of the group would maximize general utility, the utilitarian would have to endorse policies designed to suppress the unpopular religion. To raise another example, suppose that it would make a great majority extremely happy if some few persons were enslaved; suppose further that this majority is so great that their collective pleasure outweighs the collective pain of those to be enslaved. Under such conditions, the utilitarian would have to endorse slavery.[6]

In his paper on "Distributive Justice," Rawls articulates this difficulty as follows:

> [According to utilitarianism,] the percepts of justice are derivative from the one end of attaining the greatest net balance of satisfactions. There is no reason in principle why the greater gains of some should not compensate for the lesser losses of others; or why the violation of the liberty of a few might not be made right by a greater good shared by many. (*CP*, 131; cf. *TJ*, 23)

26

Because it places the good prior to the right, utilitarianism will sometimes endorse actions that will seem to us obviously unjust. Returning to our example, we are likely to think that policies which aim to suppress a particular religion violate the rights of those persons who subscribe to it, and are hence unjust, even if it is the case that such policies result in a greater sum of aggregate satisfaction. Indeed, we are likely to think that precisely what it means to have a right to free religious practice is to be entitled to practice the religion of our choice regardless of how it affects the general sum of satisfactions.[7]

It thus seems that utilitarianism cannot accommodate a robust sense of political rights; consequently, utilitarianism fails to coincide with some of our considered judgments. Specifically, we tend to believe that "each member of society has an inviolability founded on justice which even the welfare of society cannot override" and that "a loss of freedom for some is not made right by a greater sum of satisfactions enjoyed by many" (*CP*, 131; cf. *TJ*, 3 and *TJ*, 24-25); utilitarianism, it seems, cannot accommodate these judgments. On the utilitarian view, there is nothing which is *intrinsically* unjust, and there is no moral principle which is valid *in itself*; all moral principles and judgments regarding justice depend upon existing conditions in society and how they might be manipulated to produce the maximum aggregate satisfaction (*TJ*, 23). Put more generally,

> [Utilitarianism] is incapable of explaining the fact that in a just society the liberties of equal citizenship are taken for granted, and the rights secured by justice are not subject to political bargaining nor to the calculus of social interests. (*CP*, 131)

This difficulty with utilitarianism is related to another, more general problem. Because utilitarians are concerned only with maximizing the total sum of satisfaction in society, it does not matter to them how satisfaction is distributed among individuals (*TJ*, 23). To see this, let us imagine the following greatly simplified case of social distribution. Suppose that two persons, call them Smith and Jones, have one pie to distribute between themselves. There are, of course, several possible distributions; but let us limit the possibilities to the following three. On one possible distribution, the pie is cut in half, and each person receives an equal share. On another distribution, the pie is cut into quarters; Smith receives three pieces and Jones gets one. A third distribution grants Jones the entire pie, and Smith gets none. Now, we could imagine that on all three distributions, the *total sum* of satisfaction produced is equal, though distributed among Smith and Jones differently. On the first distribution, we may suppose, each individual experiences half of the total satisfaction produced by the pie.

27

On the second, Smith experiences three quarters of the satisfaction whereas Jones experiences only one quarter. In the third distribution, Smith experiences all of the satisfaction produced by the pie, and Jones experiences no satisfaction.[8]

Now, according to Rawls, the utilitarian must treat these distinct distributions as morally equivalent. What matters for the utilitarian is *how much* satisfaction is generated, not how it is distributed among persons; consequently, the utilitarian maintains that any of the three distributions is as good as any other. However, it may occur to us that there are considerations other than the sum of satisfaction which distinguish the different ways of distributing the pie. We could suppose that for some reason Jones *deserves* at least half the pie; or we might suppose that the distribution in which each individual gets half the pie is the only *fair* distribution. With either of these factors added, we might conclude that, even though the total sum of satisfaction is equal in all of the identified cases, only the first is just and the remaining two are morally unacceptable.

Of course, the utilitarian will want to reply that Jones will experience extra satisfaction knowing that he has received his just deserts or his fair share, and that this extra satisfaction is what makes the first distribution preferable to the rest. In this way, the utilitarian will translate our appeal to desert and fairness into his own language of satisfaction. However, it may nonetheless seem to us that desert and fairness are distributive concepts whose moral force is quite independent of utility; we may be inclined to think that getting what one deserves is morally important even in cases in which it does not generate the greatest possible amount of aggregate satisfaction. The utilitarian cannot account for the judgment that distributive principles that account for desert and fairness may be morally valid independent of what contribution to the production of satisfaction they might make.

Rawls states the difficulty succinctly: "utilitarianism does not take seriously the distinction between persons" (*TJ*, 24). That is, because it "adopt[s] for society as a whole the principle of rational choice for one man" (*TJ*, 24), utilitarianism cannot acknowledge any difference between Smith and Jones *as persons*. It understands all individuals to be simply subjects of satisfaction and dissatisfaction; consequently, individuals have no moral value *in themselves*. If we accept the judgments that "the rights secured by justice are not subject to political bargaining or to the calculus of social interests" (*TJ*, 4), and that distributive concepts such as desert and fairness have a moral value that is not reducible to the concept of "satisfaction," then "We shall have to look for another account of the principles of justice" (*CP*, 131).[9]

Social Contractarianism: Old and New

We began with the question, Which conception of justice is best? We have found that there is good reason to think that, despite its popularity and initial intuitive appeal, utilitarianism fails to accommodate many of our intuitive convictions and considered judgments about justice. We therefore are in need of a different theory of justice. In the history of liberal political philosophy, the rival to utilitarianism is social contractarianism. It is perhaps no surprise, then, that in formulating a new theory of liberal justice, Rawls turns to the tradition of the social contract theory. Rawls explains,

> What I have attempted to do is to generalize and carry to a higher order of abstraction the traditional theory of the social contract as represented by Locke, Rousseau, and Kant. . . . Indeed, I must disclaim any originality for the views I put forward. The leading ideas are classical and well known. (*TJ*, xviii; cf. *TJ*, 10)

We shall see that Rawls may have overstated the case with his disclaimer; despite the fact that justice as fairness is undeniably a contractarian theory, Rawls has introduced a number of innovations to the traditional doctrine. The result is a highly original theory of justice grounded in the philosophical tradition of social contractarianism.

The principal claim of traditional contractarianism is easily stated: political associations and institutions such as the state and its laws arise out of and derive their authority from an original agreement made between persons in a pre-political condition.[10] In the language of the British philosopher John Locke, an early and influential proponent of the contract view, "to understand political power right, and derive it from its original, we must consider, what state all men are naturally in" (Locke, II.4).[11] According to Locke, humans are naturally situated in a "state of nature" in which individuals are free, equal, and possessed of natural rights. Although the state of nature is a pre-political condition, it is, according to Locke, governed by a law of nature which is discoverable by reason and dictates that as all are "equal and independent, no one ought to harm another in his life, health, liberty, or possessions" (Locke, II.6). Moreover, it follows from the natural equality of all that,

> . . . the execution of the law of nature is, in [the state of nature], put into every man's hands, whereby everyone has a right to punish the transgressors of that law to such a degree, as may hinder its violation. (Locke, II.7)

29

Hence, although the state of nature is a state of perfect freedom, it is not without its inconveniences. Where each individual is responsible for enforcing the law of nature, and there is no common authoritative body to settle disputes, the natural freedom of each person is insecure and "uncertain" (Locke, IX.123). The state of nature is in this sense unstable; it easily dissolves into a "state of war," which Locke describes as a "state of *enmity* and *destruction*" (Locke, III.16) in which individuals transgress the law of nature and attempt to impose their wills upon others (Locke, III.17). It is this tendency of the state of nature to devolve into a state of war which impels individuals to enter into a social contract by which a political state will be created. Locke explains:

> To avoid this *state of war* . . . is one great reason of men's putting themselves into society, and quitting the state of nature: for where there is an authority, a power on earth, from which relief can be had by *appeal*, there the continuance of the *state of war* is excluded . . . . (Locke, III.21)

Individuals contract to generate a state for the purpose of the "mutual preservation of their lives, liberties, and estates" (Locke, IX.123). Political associations such as the state come to be when individuals agree that each shall give up a portion of his natural freedom and invest it in the state which shall henceforth function as a "judge on earth, with authority to determine all the controversies, and redress the injuries that may happen to any member of the commonwealth" (Locke, VII.89). Whereas in the state of nature, each individual held the power to execute the law of nature, in a state of society, only the political state may judge and punish. The state therefore exists for the purpose of protecting the natural rights of the individuals it governs; the state is the "umpire" which establishes "settled and standing rules" which apply equally to all individuals (Locke, VII.87).

The social contract theory is intended to address two questions fundamental to political theory: (1) Why should there be a state at all?, and (2) What kind of state should there be? Traditional contractarians explain and defend the existence of the state by an appeal to the natural, pre-political condition of humans. Since the alternative to living in political society is living in a state of nature in which one's liberties, life, and property are insecure, it is in every individual's interest to live within a state. But what *kind* of state should there be? On the contract view, a state is just only if its policies and institutions have won (or are able to win) the *consent* of its citizens. Without the consent of those it governs, the state is illegitimate and may be dissolved. Hence the social contract theory is not only an account of why there are states, it also is a test of political legitimacy. When we wish to evaluate any political body or institution, we ask, Is this arrangement one to which we have agreed? Did we contract to create this institution? If the answer to these questions is 'no', then we have good reason to think that the institution or body in question is illegitimate.

The social contract theory as traditionally stated has been subjected to forceful criticism. Among the earliest critics is Scottish philosopher, David Hume (1711-1776). Hume raises the empirical objection that states in fact arises not from mutual agreement, but through "either usurpation or conquest, or both" (Hume, 507); the social contract, Hume argues, is historically fictitious:

> The face of the earth is continually changing, by the encrease of small kingdoms into great empires, by the dissolution of great empires into smaller kingdoms, by the planting of colonies, by the migration of tribes. Is there anything discoverable in all these events, but force and violence? Where is the agreement or voluntary association so much talked of? (Hume, 508)

As there in fact never was the kind of voluntary agreement to create a society as the contractarians envision, the source of legitimate government cannot lie in a social contract. Hume further insists that, even if we were to assume for the sake of argument that at some point in the distant past individuals in a state of nature agreed to form a political society, it is unclear why such an agreement should bind *us* to the state; if our ancestors entered into a social contract by which our present government exists, this original contract "cannot now be supposed to retain any authority" (Hume, 507). Hence it appears that the entire strategy of social contractarianism fails.

Contractarians have responded to these empirical objections by insisting that the social contract is not intended to provide an historical explanation of the origin of political society. The point of the contract theory is to promote a *way of thinking* about politics; the social contract is to be understood as a *hypothetical* agreement.[12] When evaluating political arrangements, we are to ask, Would we have agreed to this, if given the choice? Are these the institutions that we would have consented to create in the state of nature? In this way, the contractarian avoids Hume's concern with historical accuracy. Political arrangements are just if they are such as we would have agreed to them in a *hypothetical* original agreement.

However, it is not clear that this shift towards a *hypothetical* social contract accomplishes much. Does the fact that we *would have* consented to some political policy or institution under certain *hypothetical* conditions justify that policy or institution under *actual* conditions? Can a *hypothetical* agreement have any justificatory force in the real world? In an oft-cited passage, Ronald Dworkin makes the point in this way, "A hypothetical contract is not simply a pale form of an actual contract, it is no contract at all" (Dworkin 1973, 18). Again, it seems that the social contract theory fails to provide any plausible account of the legitimacy of political arrangements.

Under the force of objections similar to those raised by Hume, social contractarianism languished throughout most of the twentieth century. In *A Theory of* Justice, Rawls revives the contractarian approach. However, Rawls's contractarianism differs from the traditional theory in significant respects. Chief among these is that Rawls puts the device of the social contract to a purpose which is different from that of the traditional contractarians. Whereas the traditional theorists employed the contract theory to try to explain the source of political legitimacy and obligation, Rawls maintains that "we are not to think of the original contract as one to enter a particular society or to set up a particular form of government" (*TJ*, 10). Rawls's primary aim is not that of explaining the origin and legitimacy of political association; he rather aims to propose a framework which can explain and organize our considered judgments concerning justice in a way which may serve as a guide for further political decision. The main contention of *A Theory of Justice* is that "the conception of justice that is implicit in the contract tradition" is the one which "best approximates our considered judgments of justice and constitutes the most appropriate moral basis for a democratic society" (*TJ*, xviii).

In *A Theory of Justice*, then, the idea of an original contract serves as an "expository device" (*TJ*, 19); it takes the form of what philosophers call a "thought experiment," an exercise in which one places certain artificial or hypothetical constraints upon one's thinking in an effort to identify, clarify, and systematize one's own common sense judgments.[13] Rawls thus does not follow Locke and the traditional contractarians in directing us to consider "what state all men are naturally in" (Locke, II.4), he rather asks us to imaginatively place ourselves in a condition specially designed to aid us in thinking about justice. In this way, Rawls's version of the "state of nature," which Rawls calls the "original position" (*TJ*, 11), is not to be understood as a model of the "natural condition" of human beings, and is therefore not to be mistaken for an historical or anthropological *explanation* of how societies arise and from whence their authority derives. Indeed, Rawls's version of the contract theory does not attempt to *explain* anything; it is rather device designed to help us think more clearly about justice.

Thus far, we have examined Rawls's reasons for rejecting the dominant theory of justice of his time. We have also said something about the *kind* of alternate theory Rawls wishes to propose. Now we may turn to a general exposition of justice as fairness, Rawls's positive account of justice.

The Basics of Justice as Fairness

Choosing Justice

Justice as fairness begins with a roughly contractarian scenario. We are to imagine hypothetical persons (Rawls calls them "parties") in an "original position" who are "free and rational" and "concerned to further their own interests" choosing together, in "one joint act," a conception of justice which will "assign basic rights and duties" and "determine the division of social benefits" (*TJ*, 10). This conception of justice will in turn "regulate all further agreements" among the parties and also "specify the kinds of social cooperation that can be entered into and the forms of government that can be established" (*TJ*, 10). Hence, on Rawls's view, the agreement reached in the original position does not establish a constitution or a form of government; rather, the subject of the agreement, *what is agreed to*, is something more basic:

> Justice as fairness begins . . . with one of the most general of
> all choices which persons might make together, namely, with
> the choice of the first principles of a conception of justice
> which is to regulate all subsequent criticism and reform of
> institutions. Then, having chosen a conception of justice, we
> can suppose that they are to choose a constitution and a
> legislature to enact laws, and so on, all in accordance with the
> principles of justice initially agreed upon. (*TJ*, 11-12)

Thus the agreement in the original position, once decided upon, establishes "once and for all" what social justice is (*TJ*, 11); that is, parties to the original agreement decide upon the "first principles" of justice which shall condition all other aspects of social life and organization.

33

The Original Position and the Veil of Ignorance

As its influence on society is far-reaching, the agreement made in the original position is monumental. The conception of justice that is chosen will affect the lives of all parties, and, we may suppose, the lives of their ancestors. Here we might want to consider an objection often brought against traditional contractarian theories: won't the principles of justice chosen in the original position simply reflect the interests of the most powerful or otherwise advantaged parties? If we accept that the parties in the original position are "concerned to further their own interests," (*TJ*, 10) and, furthermore, that the interests of one person may conflict with those of another, it follows that any agreement will involve compromise and bargaining among the parties. It is natural to suppose that some parties in the original position will occupy an advantaged position from which to bargain. For example, certain parties will be more clever, better informed, or more prudent than others; some may have more foresight and be able to better predict how a given conception of justice will affect their own prospects. In short, we may worry that the agreement made in the original position is likely to privilege some parties at the expense of the interests of others; the original position may turn out to be *unfair*.

To meet this traditional objection, Rawls introduces a concept new to contractarianism. On Rawls's view, the principles of justice are not chosen from a Lockean state of nature in which self-interested individuals bargain for social arrangements agreeable to their own interests; Rawls builds into his conception of the original position a feature which he calls the "veil of ignorance" (*TJ*, 11).[14] The veil of ignorance deprives the contracting parties of information about themselves and their particular interests and desires. More specifically, in Rawls's original position,

> No one knows his place in society, his class position or social
> status, nor does any one know his fortune in the distribution of
> natural assets and abilities, his intelligence, strength, and the
> like. (*TJ*, 11; cf. *TJ*, 118)

Rawls additionally stipulates that the veil of ignorance deprives the parties of information about their "conceptions of the good" and their "special psychological propensities" (*TJ*, 11). In this way, the veil of ignorance corrects for "the arbitrariness of the world" (*TJ*, 122) by guaranteeing that "no one is advantaged or disadvantaged in the choice of principles by the outcome of natural chance or the contingency of social circumstances" (*TJ*, 11). Although the parties in the original position are rational and self-interested, the veil nullifies "the effects of specific contingencies which put men at odds and tempt them to exploit social and natural circumstances to their own advantage" (*TJ*, 118). Since the veil of ignorance ensures that "no one knows his situation in society nor his assets," none of the parties is "in a position to tailor principles to his advantage"; hence there is "no basis for bargaining" in the original position (*TJ*, 120-121). Therefore, the conception of justice that emerges from the original position is "the result of a fair agreement" (*TJ*, 11).

By blocking out "those aspects of the social world that seem arbitrary from a moral point of view" (*TJ*, 14), the veil of ignorance ensures that any agreement made in the original position will be fair. We now see the connection between justice and fairness that Rawls's view suggests. Justice as fairness is the view which asserts that any principles of justice that would be agreed to by free, rational, and self-interested parties situated behind a veil of ignorance are *ipso facto* just; conversely, any principles which could not be agreed to by such parties are *ipso facto* unjust. More generally stated, according to justice as fairness, any principle agreed to under fair conditions of deliberation and choice is a just principle. Hence the name, "justice as fairness."

Before moving on, it is important to emphasize again that the original position is intended to function as a thought experiment. That is, Rawls is not offering an historical, anthropological, or psychological explanation of how conceptions of justice arise; rather, he is proposing a theoretical framework within which to think about justice and a perspective from which to evaluate different conceptions of justice.[15] As Rawls says,

> . . . one or more persons can at any time enter [the original] position, or perhaps better, simulate the deliberations of this hypothetical situation, simply by reasoning in accordance with the appropriate restrictions. (*TJ*, 119)

Here we might ask, Why should we think about justice in this way? Why should we accept the "restrictions" on our thinking about justice represented by the veil of ignorance? Perhaps you have anticipated Rawls's response: "the conditions embodied in the description of the original position are ones that we do in fact accept" (*TJ*, 19; cf. *TJ*, 514); the original position "best expresses the conditions that are widely thought reasonable to impose on the choice of principles" (*TJ*, 105), it collects together "into one conception a number of conditions on principles that we are ready upon due consideration to recognize as reasonable" (*TJ*, 19). In short, Rawls holds that his approach to justice best matches out considered judgments.

Indeed, it seems that Rawls's original position does fit many of our considered judgments. To see this, employ the method of analysis we used in our earlier discussion of utilitarianism: consider a proposal that seems obviously unjust, and see whether it could be endorsed on Rawls's view. For example, the proposal that special social advantages should be given to persons with blonde hair and green eyes would never be chosen by rational and self-interested parties in the original position. Recall that behind the veil of ignorance, no one knows the color of his hair and eyes; thus no one concerned to advance his own interests could agree to such a proposal. Of course, this is an artificial example; we could, however, consider similar proposals recommending that basic liberties be distributed according to skin color, sex, intelligence, or religious conviction. As the parties in the original position do not know their skin color, sex, level of intelligence, or religious convictions, such proposals would not be chosen, and are therefore, according to Rawls's view, unjust. For another kind of example, consider the proposal that persons of exceptional musical ability should rule over all others. Again, as no one in the original position knows the level of his musical ability, such a principle would not be chosen and is therefore unjust. Finally, consider that the parties in the original position would not agree to a conception of justice which allows slavery or other forms of forced servitude. In these and in other cases, Rawls's view seems to accommodate our considered judgments.

Motivation: The Thin Theory of the Good

The last section ended with a brief discussion of what kind of principles could not be chosen in the original position. We saw that racist, sexist, and other forms of discriminatory or arbitrary policies are unjust according to Rawls's theory. In this respect, Rawls's approach to justice corresponds with our intuitive judgments. However, there is a problem lurking which we shall call the "problem of motivation." In showing that the proposal for slavery would not be chosen in the original position and hence is unjust, we relied upon the intuition that no one would want to be a slave. However, it is not clear that this kind of reasoning is available to the parties in the original position. Since the veil of ignorance excludes knowledge of one's beliefs about what is good and what is desirable, it seems there is no motivation to choose any particular principle of justice rather than any other. To see this, imagine yourself in a restaurant with an extensive dinner menu. How

shall you decide which items to order? Typically, your decision would
be based upon such factors as your appetite, your desires, how much
money you want to spend, and what kinds of food you like. Your
choice to order, say, a hamburger, will be motivated by factors such as
your desire for a hamburger, your knowledge that you can afford to
purchase a hamburger, etc. Now imagine yourself behind the veil of
ignorance, temporarily deprived of knowledge of your own tastes,
appetites, preferences, and desires. Is it possible to *choose* a meal from
behind the veil of ignorance? The concept of a *choice* implies that the
chooser has some criteria according to which he ranks the possible
dinner selections which *motivate* him to choose one option over the
others. However, the veil of ignorance blocks all such motivating
criteria. Therefore we might say that one cannot *choose* a meal from
behind the veil of ignorance; since there are no criteria upon which
choice may be based, the selection of a meal is not motivated by
anything. All that is possible is a near random selection from the menu.

Therefore the veil of ignorance blocks the kind of information
which would cause one to reject principles of justice which are racist,
sexist or otherwise discriminatory. Due to the veil of ignorance, a
person in the original position does not know that he prefers to not be
discriminated against or enslaved; he therefore has no reason to reject
the proposal which recommends slavery. Generalizing the point, we
may say that, from behind the veil of ignorance, there is no reason to
prefer any conception of justice to any other; there is nothing
motivating the choice of principles of justice. Under such conditions,
there is no *choice* in the proper sense, but only what may be called
"guesswork" or random selection (*TJ*, 123).

To meet this problem, Rawls introduces what he calls the "thin
theory of the good" (*TJ*, 348). We are to suppose that there are certain
"primary goods" which "normally have a use whatever a person's
rational plan of life" (*TJ*, 54). Primary goods are things "that every
rational man is presumed to want" (*TJ*, 54), "whatever else he wants"
(*TJ*, 79). Among these goods are particular social goods such as "rights,
liberties, and opportunities, and income, and wealth," and "self-
respect" (*TJ*, 54).[16] According to the thin theory of the good, parties in
the original position know what these primary social goods are and they
"assume that they normally prefer more primary goods rather than less"
(*TJ*, 123). Parties want more rather than less of the primary goods
because,

> With more of these goods men can generally be assured of
> greater success in carrying out their intentions and in
> advancing their ends, whatever these ends may be. (*TJ*, 79)

37

With the thin theory of the good postulated, Rawls concludes:

> Thus even though the parties are deprived of information
> about their particular ends, they have enough knowledge to
> rank the alternatives. They know that in general they must try
> to protect their liberties, widen their opportunities, and enlarge
> their means for promoting their aims whatever these are.
> Guided by the theory of the good . . . their deliberations are no
> longer guesswork. They can make a rational decision in the
> ordinary sense. (*TJ*, 123)

The thin theory of the good resolves the motivation problem. Rational persons situated behind the veil of ignorance do not know their own aspirations, preferences, and values, but they do know that human beings are generally better able to realize their individual aspirations and satisfy their individual preferences if their lives contain more primary goods rather than less. Hence they are able to deliberate and choose principles of justice in a manner which is typical of rational persons under normal circumstances. That is, given the thin theory of the good, a person in the original position has,

> . . . a coherent set of preferences between the options open to
> him. He ranks these options according to how well they
> further his purposes; he follows the plan which will satisfy
> more of his desires rather than less, and which has the greater
> chance of being successfully executed. (*TJ*, 124)

To complete our characterization of the original position, we must note two additional motivational assumptions Rawls adopts in order to help simplify the original position. The first of these is that the parties in the original position are not motivated by envy. That is, a person in the original position "is not ready to accept a loss for himself if only others have less as well"; "He is not downcast by the knowledge or perception that others have a larger index of primary social goods" (*TJ*, 124). The second assumption is that the parties "are presumed to have a sense of justice and this fact is public knowledge among them" (*TJ*, 125). Because of this sense of justice, "the parties can rely on each other to understand and to act in accordance with whatever principles are finally chosen"; hence the parties know that "their undertaking is not in vain" (*TJ*, 125).

With these motivational assumptions in place, we may summarize the idea of the original position as follows:

> . . . the persons in the original position try to acknowledge
> principles which advance their system of ends as far as
> possible. They do this by attempting to win for themselves the

highest index of primary social goods, since this enables them to promote their conception of the good most effectively whatever it turns out to be. The parties do not seek to confer benefits or to impose injuries on one another; they are not moved by affection or rancor. Nor do they try to gain relative to each other; they are not envious or vain. (*TJ*, 125)

Presentation of the Alternatives and the Strategy of Choice

With the original position characterized as such, Rawls next asks us to imagine that the parties in the original position are presented with a list of conceptions of justice from which to choose. The list, which is presented on page 107 of *A Theory of Justice*, includes many of the standard philosophical conceptions of justice, including various utilitarian proposals as well as Rawls's own favored conception of justice (to be examined in the next section). Of course, Rawls admits that his list is not exhaustive; it does not contain all possible conceptions of justice, but rather the philosophical options which traditionally have been most influential. The parties "are presented with this list and required to agree unanimously that one conception is best among those enumerated" (*TJ*, 106). And remember the principal claim of justice as fairness: whatever conception of justice would be chosen in the original position is *ipso facto* the best conception of justice.

We have made repeated reference to the "deliberation" and "reasoning" of the parties behind the veil of ignorance; we have said that each party to the decision in the original position seeks to further his own interests. Yet the question remains, How shall the parties rank the options? What strategy of choice shall they employ? We could imagine the parties adopting the strategy which instructs them to rank the options according to the best possible outcome, and select that conception of justice in which the very best off in society are better off than they would be under any alternative conception. Alternatively, one could imagine a strategy which directs the parties to rank the options according to the likely outcome for the greatest number of persons, and choose that conception of justice which maximizes the share of primary social goods for the greatest number of persons possible.

Rawls argues that neither of the above strategies of choice would be employed by rational parties in the original position. Whereas the first strategy identified above directs the parties to assume the position of the very best off in society, and the second strategy instructs them to adopt the view of the average person in society, the strategy which Rawls maintains the parties would adopt requires them to assume the perspective of the very worst off in society. That is, Rawls argues that parties in the original position would adopt the decision strategy known as *maximin*.[17] The maximin principle "tells us to rank alternatives by their worst possible outcomes: we are to adopt the alternative the worst outcome of which is superior to the worst outcomes of the others" (*TJ*, 133); we may thus say that the maximin rule directs us to maximize the minimum outcome. As he puts it in his 1958 paper, "Justice as Fairness," a rational person in the original position chooses principles of justice as if he was "designing a practice in which his enemy were to assign him his place" (*CP*, 54).[18]

The especially conservative and cautious attitude recommended by the maximin strategy might strike us as unusually restrictive; Rawls acknowledges that it is "not, in general, a suitable guide for choices" (*TJ*, 133). However, there are certain conditions under which the maximin strategy is in fact the most rational decision rule (*TJ*, 134). Rawls's arguments that the conditions represented by the original position require the maximin strategy have generated significant controversy among commentators and we shall not review them here.[19] Consider only that if the maximin strategy is indeed adopted by the parties in the original position, they will not choose a conception of justice which recommends the maximization of average utility; that is, if one accepts Rawls's motivational and choice-theoretic stipulations, one must reject utilitarianism.

Two Principles of Justice

What conception of justice *would* be chosen in the original position? The bulk of *A Theory of Justice* is devoted to the demonstration of the claim that free and rational parties concerned to further their own interests would choose exactly two principles of justice in the original position. These two principles are therefore, on Rawls's view, the correct principles of justice. There are several formulations of these principles in *A Theory of Justice*. Here are Rawls's final formulations:

First Principle of Justice

> Each person is to have an equal right to the most extensive total system of equal basic liberties compatible with a similar system of liberty for all.

Second Principle of Justice

> Social and economic inequalities are to be arranged so that they are both:(a) to the greatest benefit of the least advantaged ... , and (b) attached to offices and positions open to all under conditions of fair equality of opportunity.[20] (*TJ*, 266)

To fix terms, we may refer to the first principle as the "liberty principle"; while the first part of the second principle is known as the "difference principle" and the second part is called the "equal opportunity principle."

Rawls argues further that rational parties would agree to two priority rules by which the principles are to be ranked when conflicts arise. The first priority rule establishes that the Liberty Principle has priority over the second principle of justice; this means that liberty guaranteed by the first principle cannot be sacrificed for social and economic gains (*TJ*, 55). According to the second priority rule, the equal opportunity principle has priority over the difference principle.

In recent work, Rawls has reformulated the principles as follows:

First Principle of Justice

> Each person has an equal claim to a fully adequate scheme of equal basic rights and liberties, which scheme is compatible with the same scheme for all; and in this scheme the equal political liberties, and only those liberties, are to be guaranteed their fair value.

Second Principle of Justice

> Social and economic inequalities are to satisfy two conditions: first, they are to be attached to positions and offices open to all under conditions of fair equality of opportunity; second, they are to be to the greatest benefit of the least advantaged members of society.[21] (*PL*, 5-6)

The two principles express a "general conception" of justice:

> All social primary goods—liberty , opportunity, income, and wealth, and the bases of self-respect—are to be distributed equally unless an unequal distribution of any or all of these goods is to the advantage of the least favored.[22]

41

It follows from this general conception that injustice is inequality that is not to everyone's advantage (*TJ*, 54).

These are sophisticated principles of justice, and their precise interpretation, especially with regard to the difference principle, is a matter of dispute. I shall, however, offer the following brief explanations of Rawls's principles.

The Liberty Principle

Among Rawls's principles of justice, the liberty principle is the easiest to interpret. The liberty principle stipulates that every person is equally entitled to a system of equal basic liberties, and that the liberty conferred by this system is to be as extensive as possible. The basic liberties Rawls has in mind are those typical of a liberal approach to political philosophy:

> Important among these are political liberty (the right to vote and to hold public office) and freedom of speech and assembly; liberty of conscience and freedom of thought; freedom of the person, which includes freedom from psychological oppression and physical assault . . . ; the right to hold personal property and freedom from arbitrary arrest and seizure . . . . (*TJ*, 53)

Rawls's first principle of justice stipulates that these basic liberties are distributed equally among all individuals. "The only reason for circumscribing basic liberties and making them less extensive is that otherwise they would interfere with one another" (*TJ*, 56).

The Equal Opportunity Principle

The equal opportunity principle can be easily explained. Whereas the difference principle guarantees that distributive inequalities benefit the least advantaged, the equal opportunity principle requires that the offices and positions which may generate economic and social advantages be open to all. Most basically stated, the equal opportunity principle establishes "equal life prospects in all sectors of society for those similarly endowed and motivated" (*TJ*, 265). This principle is more demanding than it may seem. For it demands not only that positions and offices be "open to all" in the formal sense, but also that political institutions take positive steps to ensure that persons with similar skills and motivation enjoy similar opportunities. As Rawls explains:

> ... equality of opportunity means a certain set of institutions that assures similar chances of education and culture for persons similarly motivated and keeps positions and offices open to all on the basis of qualities and efforts reasonably related to the relevant duties and tasks. (*TJ*, 245-246)

The Difference Principle

Rawls's difference principle is the subject of much controversy among political theorists. The first thing to note is that, according to Rawls, social and economic inequalities are not necessarily unjust; in fact, the difference principle will in may cases *require* unequal distributions of social and economic resources. Rawls is in this sense not a strict egalitarian. However, Rawls is also not a standard *laissez faire* capitalist; he is not content to leave all distributive questions to the free market. The difference principle requires government intervention within the social and economic order. Specifically, it requires that inequalities must be eliminated except in cases where they are to the benefit of those worst off in society. Of course, a more detailed explanation is needed. To simplify matters, let us leave aside the vexed question of what constitutes "social inequality" and how this is to be gauged.[23] Instead, let us concentrate on an example of economic distribution.

We are to distribute economic resources to three men, Smith, Jones, and Adams. The difference principle stipulates that resources must be distributed equally unless there is an unequal distribution in which the person least well off is better off than he would be under the equal distribution. Put a different way, the difference principle requires that if there is an unequal distribution under which the lot of the worst off is better than it would be under an equal distribution, then this unequal distribution should be adopted. Moreover, if there are several unequal distributions under which the lot of the worst off is better than it would be under an equal distribution, then we must implement that unequal distribution under which the lot of the worst off is *most* improved over the equal distribution.

Consider the following chart of different possible distributions among Smith, Jones, and Adams.[24] The numbers represent shares of economic resources; we presume that a greater share is better than an lesser share.

	A	B	C	D	E
Smith	10	20	20	15	15
Jones	10	5	10	20	18
Adams	10	5	10	12	14

Distribution A represents the equal distribution. Suppose that the only alternative to A is B; implementing distribution B is unjust according to the difference principle since it grants Smith a gain in resources which does not also benefit Jones and Adams. Distribution C grants the same gain to Smith as B, but it leaves Jones and Adams with the same share as they would have under A; the difference principle disallows this distribution since it is an unequal distribution which does not benefit the worst off (in this case, Jones and Adams are both the worst off). Distribution D grants a gain to Jones, but suppose that in granting these additional resources to Jones, the holdings of Smith and Adams are improved as well. We might imagine that Jones is especially inventive, and, with the appropriate economic resources, can generate additional resources which can then be redistributed to Smith and Adams. According to the difference principle, distribution D is just if the only other options are A, B, and C. Now consider distribution E. E grants a lesser gain to Jones than D, yet it confers a greater benefit to Adams, who is in this case the worst off. According to the difference principle, distribution E is the most just of the distributions identified.

Of course, the above illustration should not be taken too literally. Rawls, after all, intends the difference principle to govern those basic social institutions which allocate all social primary goods other than basic liberty; the difference principle applies to institutions that distribute wealth, status, and authority. Moreover, Rawls stipulates that the difference principle is to evaluate distributions among what he calls "representative persons" (*TJ*, 56), which are perhaps best understood as socio-economic classes rather than as individual persons. Thus, we should think of Smith, Jones and Adams not as persons, but rather as "representative men," that is, exemplars of distinct social and economic groups.[25] Rawls explains:

> The difference principle is a very special criterion: it applies primarily to the basic structure of society via representative individuals whose expectations are to be estimated by an index of primary goods. (*TJ*, 72)

44

Let us now consider a concrete example of how the difference principle may be applied. Philosopher Allen Buchanan provides a standard kind of case:

> Suppose that large-scale capital investment in a certain industry is required to raise employment and to produce new goods and services. Suppose that by raising employment and producing these new goods and services such capital investment will ultimately be of great benefit to the least advantaged members of the society. Suppose in particular, that such capital investment, if it can be achieved, will greatly increase the income prospects of the least advantaged through employing many who are not now employed and by raising the wages of those who are already employed. Suppose, however, that individuals will not be willing to undertake the risks of this large-scale capital investment unless they have the opportunity to reap large profits from the enterprise, should it succeed. In such a case, tax advantages for capital investment and lowered taxes on profits might provide the needed incentives for investment.[26] (Buchanan 1980, 11)

Under these conditions, the difference principle would require the institution of a tax policy which provides the kind of incentives necessary to encourage investment. This policy would constitute an unequal distribution of the tax burden, and would, if the investment it encourages is successful, lead to an unequal distribution in wealth. However, these inequalities are justified provided they may be reasonably expected to improve the prospects for the least advantaged members of society.

There is a further dimension of the difference principle which is worthy of note before moving on. It might seem that the difference principle corrects for the kinds of contingencies which may lead to one person having a greater share of economic resources than he deserves. So, for example, if you happen to have been born into a very wealthy, upper class family, the difference principle places certain constraints on the kinds of advantages you can derive from your good fortune. In this regard, the difference principle has a certain intuitive appeal; it is by luck that you were born into your socio-economic position. Strictly speaking, you do not *deserve* the benefits that come with that position. The difference principle accordingly redistributes wealth and other social advantages which arise from luck.

The difference principle may loose some of its intuitive appeal, however, when we consider advantages that arise from talents and natural endowments. Rawls proposes to treat inequalities arising from

45

differences in natural endowments among individuals as he would treat those arising from contingencies of birth; "from a moral standpoint, both seem equally arbitrary" (*TJ*, 65). Rawls thus maintains that persons born with exceptional ingenuity, or intelligence, or beauty do not, strictly speaking, *deserve* their endowments, and hence do not *deserve* the social and economic advantages that they may generate. When someone does gain an advantage due to his talent or natural abilities, the difference principle requires compensation; accordingly, advantages will be redistributed in the way prescribed by the difference principle. Rawls writes, "Those who have been favored by nature, whoever they are, may gain from their good fortune only on terms that improve the situation of those who have lost out" (*TJ*, 87).

We might wonder, as many critics have, how it follows from the fact that I do not deserve the benefits arising from my natural abilities and talents that these benefits are to be distributed to the advantage of the worst off in society.[27] Even if it is granted that I do not deserve the advantages that are generated by my natural abilities, it does not immediately follow that these advantages are deserved by anyone else, much less the least advantaged. Anticipating this concern, Rawls explains:

> The difference principle represents, in effect, an agreement to regard the distribution of natural talents as in some respects a common asset and to share in the greater social and economic benefits made possible by the complementarities of this distribution. (*TJ*, 87)

Hence the difference principle does not only prescribe a certain pattern of distribution of social primary goods, it also suggests a way of *thinking* about desert on the basis of which the basic structure of society should be organized. By way of summary, Rawls writes:

> No one deserves his greater natural capacity nor merits a more favorable starting place in society. But, of course, this is no reason to ignore, much less to eliminate these distinctions. Instead, the basic structure can be arranged so that these contingencies work for the good of the least fortunate. Thus we are led to the difference principle if we wish to set up the social system so that no one gains or loses from his arbitrary place in the distribution of natural assets or his initial position in society without giving or receiving compensating advantages in return. (*TJ*, 87)

Justice as Fairness: Criticism and Controversy

Having completed our sketch of justice as fairness, let us turn to some of the more important lines of criticism to emerge at the time of the publication of *A Theory of Justice*. It is widely believed that it is in part due to these criticisms that Rawls introduced certain revisions and qualifications to justice as fairness in his subsequent work. Rawls's later elaborations of justice as fairness, as presented in his *Political Liberalism*, will be examined in the next chapter.[28] Here, we shall briefly survey some of the criticisms that helped precipitate Rawls's revisions.

Liberal philosophers generally sympathetic to Rawls's two principles of justice have raised concerns about Rawls's methodology and the completeness of his theory. To understand these worries, let us return to a point touched upon earlier. Assume that the hypothetical parties in the original position would choose Rawls's two principles. According to justice as fairness, it follows from the fact that Rawls's two principles would be chosen in the original position that they are the correct principles of justice. Why should this be? What is the nature of the supposed connection between choice-worthiness in the original position and justice such that any principle chosen in the original position is *ipso facto* a valid principle of justice? As Rawls's theory seems to rely on there being such a relationship, one may reasonably expect Rawls to provide a philosophical account of this connection; however, Rawls does not provide such an account in *A Theory of Justice*.

Consider the response that such questions and concerns are misplaced. Rawls may reply that justice as fairness does not rely upon any philosophical connection between choice in the original position and justice; the idea of an agreement in the original position simply helps us to "see" or conceptualize the idea of justice that we already intuitively endorse. Hence we might say that, in *A Theory of Justice*, Rawls does not *argue* for a conception of justice; he rather *presupposes* a general conception of justice and proposes a *way of thinking* about justice, what might be called a *theoretical model* of justice, that helps us to better organize and prioritize our considered judgments.

This kind of response will satisfy for as long as we never question the soundness of our considered judgments and the correctness of our intuitive conception of justice. Is it not possible that our intuitions and considered judgments are ultimately unreliable guides to justice? The critics may thus respond that a theory of justice must amount to more than a model of our intuitive ideas about justice. After all, they may continue, we want to know *what justice is*, not simply what we are inclined to *believe* justice is or what our considered judgments *suggest* justice is. A properly philosophical theory of justice must attempt to demonstrate the *truth* or *correctness* of a given conception of justice.

If we accept this idea of what a proper theory of justice is, we will have to conclude that Rawls's *A Theory of Justice* does not present a "theory" in the strict sense of the term, and is therefore incomplete. Hence the philosopher Thomas Nagel, in his 1973 review of *A Theory of Justice*, writes,

> The egalitarian liberalism which [Rawls] develops and the conception of the good on which it depends are extremely persuasive, but the original position serves to model, rather than to justify them . . . . I believe that Rawls' conclusions can be more persuasively defended by direct moral arguments for liberty and equality. (Nagel 1973, 15)

Ronald Dworkin, in his review of Rawls, expresses a similar concern:

> [Rawls's] two principles comprise a theory of justice that is built up from the hypothesis of a contract. But the contract sensibly cannot be taken as the fundamental premise or postulate of that theory . . . . It must be seen as a kind of halfway point in a larger argument, as itself the product of a deeper political theory . . . . We must therefore try to identify the features of a deeper theory that would recommend the device of a contract as the engine of justice . . . . (Dworkin 1973, 37)

Dworkin and Nagel both allude to the incompleteness of *A Theory of Justice*. Maintaining that the argument from the original position is insufficient, Nagel calls for "direct moral arguments" for Rawls's principles; such arguments, he contends, would be more persuasive than Rawls's own account. Dworkin is likewise not satisfied with Rawls's contractarian arguments for his principles; Dworkin interprets the fundamental features of justice as fairness such as the original position and the veil of ignorance to be the *products* of some unstated and "deeper" political philosophy which can be excavated and evaluated independently of Rawls's account.

Nagel and Dworkin think that Rawls's principles of justice need further justification, and that the ultimate test of Rawls's principles lies in the strength of the "direct moral arguments" (Nagel 1973,15) that can be marshaled to support Rawls's "deep theory" (Dworkin 1973, 51). If we are to evaluate Rawls's theory, then, we must set aside the contractarian elements of justice as fairness and search for the philosophical claims which it presupposes as its foundation. If these claims turn out to be philosophically defensible, then we may accept justice as fairness as an especially useful portrait of justice rather than a theory of justice in its own right. If, however, the philosophical foundations of justice as fairness turn out to be weak or dubious, we shall have to abandon Rawls's account of justice as well as the "deep theory" it is based upon.

One critic who opposes liberalism itself has attempted to unearth the deeper philosophical views underlying *A Theory of Justice*. In his book-length critique of Rawls, *Liberalism and the Limits of Justice*,[29] Michael Sandel argues that justice as fairness presupposes a philosophical conception of the self which is demonstrably false.[30] According to Sandel, the construct of the original position commits Rawls to the view that the self is essentially an asocial *chooser* of its aspirations, values, and aims. That is, Sandel contends that Rawls is committed to the view that "what is most essential to our personhood is not the ends we choose but our capacity to choose them" (Sandel 1998, 19). On this interpretation, the veil of ignorance is a device by which the self is stripped of everything but its most essential characteristic, namely, its ability to make a choice. Principles of justice chosen from behind the veil of ignorance may then be seen as expressions of human nature in its purest form. In a passage which lends considerable support to Sandel's interpretation, Rawls explains:

> It is not our aims that primarily reveal our nature but rather the
> principles that we would acknowledge to govern the
> background conditions under which these aims are to be found
> and the manner in which they are to be pursued. For the self is
> prior to the ends which are affirmed by it . . . . (*TJ*, 491)

Sandel argues that it is this image of the autonomous chooser, what he calls the "unencumbered self" (Sandel 1998, 180), that lies at the heart of justice as fairness.[31] Should this theory of the self turn out to be false, we will have good reason to abandon Rawls's theory of justice.

Indeed, Sandel argues that "the image of the unencumbered self is flawed" (Sandel 1996, 13). According to Sandel, if the self is essentially a chooser of its ends, it must be "prior" to them and consequently stand "always at a certain distance" (Sandel 1998, 10) from its own values and aims. That is, on the Rawlsian picture, my deepest values and aspirations, the ends to which I have dedicated my life, my most fundamental convictions about how I ought to live, "are *mine* rather than *me*"; they are "things I *have* rather than *am*" (Sandel 1998, 85). This conception of the self entails that,

49

No commitment could grip me so deeply that I could not understand myself without it. No transformation of life purposes and plans could be so unsettling as to disrupt the contours of my identity. No project could be so essential that turning away from it would call into question the person I am. (Sandel 1998, 62)

However, Sandel argues that the image of the unencumbered self "fails to capture those loyalties and responsibilities whose moral force consists partly in the fact that living by them is inseparable from understanding ourselves as the particular persons we are" (Sandel 1996, 14; cf. Sandel 1998, 179). Certain obligations, Sandel contends, are such that they cannot be properly understood as the product of the choice of an unencumbered self. For example, the force of religious, familial, and patriotic duties and loyalties lies precisely in the fact that these are compulsory and not voluntary. That is, some of my ends are not simply *mine*, but *me*; at the most fundamental levels, my commitments are not separable from *who I am*, they are *constitutive* of my identity. Moreover, it is often the case that such constitutive commitments are necessary to our self-understandings; we are not essentially asocial choosers of our own ends, but always the bearers of certain social ties and relations. Sandel hence promotes the somewhat Aristotelian view that selves are essentially socially "encumbered" by the relations they bear to other selves and groups of selves. That is, on Sandel's view, we are essentially "members of this family or community or nation or people . . . bearers of this history . . . sons and daughters of that revolution . . . citizens of this republic" (Sandel 1998, 179). As the philosopher Alasdair MacIntyre has said, "I am born with a past" (MacIntyre, 221), and that past in part determines who I am.

The theory of the unencumbered self cannot make sense of these most important and "indispensable aspects of our moral and political experience" (Sandel 1996, 14), and is for this reason an inadequate basis for a theory of justice. However, Sandel's criticism extends further. In addition to his critique of the theory of the unencumbered self which underlies justice as fairness, Sandel contends also that Rawls covertly employs the conception of a socially encumbered self in his depiction of the difference principle (Sandel 1998, 80).

Recall that the difference principle stipulates that economic and social goods other than basic liberty are to be distributed so that inequalities are to the advantage of the least well-off in society. Recall also that, according to Rawls, this scheme of distribution "represents, in effect, an agreement to regard the distribution of natural talents as in some respects a common asset" (*TJ*, 87). Sandel argues that there is no basis for regarding the natural distribution of individual talents a "common asset" unless we "presuppose some prior moral tie" among individuals (Sandel 1984b, 22). However, on the theory of the unencumbered self, there are no such prior ties which could justify regarding an individual's natural talents as a common asset. Sandel concludes that Rawls's theory of justice is "parasitic" on the kind of theory of the self that it "officially rejects" (Sandel 1998, 80). In short, Sandel argues that Rawls presupposes a theory of the self which is not only false, but insufficient for his own purposes.

Sandel's objections have seemed to many quite forceful. If Sandel's argument that the justice as fairness presupposes the theory of the unencumbered self, then Rawls's theory of justice must confront what appear to be very serious problems. Rawls must show either that the unencumbered self is not incompatible with the difference principle or that justice as fairness is not committed to the philosophical presuppositions that Sandel has identified. Rawls's work following *A Theory of Justice* has been focused on the task of clarifying and reformulating justice as fairness. In the next chapter, we shall examine Rawls's restatement of justice as fairness as formulated in his second major work in political philosophy, *Political Liberalism.*

Endnotes

[1] See also Rawls's 1967 paper, "Distributive Justice" (*CP*, 130-153), which begins with a similar statement.

[2] The term "hedonism" derives from the Greek word for "pleasure" (*hedonê*). The utilitarian philosopher, Jeremy Bentham (1748-1832) states the hedonistic thesis thus: "*Evil* is pain, or the cause of pain. *Good* is pleasure or the cause of pleasure" (Bentham 1789, 685); see also Mill 1991, 137. More sophisticated utilitarians substitute terms such as "satisfaction" for Bentham's "pleasure"; see, for example, Sidgwick; Hare 1981; Shaw; and Smart. In the discussion that follows, I shall use "satisfaction," and "utility" interchangeably.

[3] Compare Rawls's "Distributive Justice" (*CP*, 130-131).

[4] For further discussion of this, see Sandel 1998, 2-7.

[5] See, for example, John Stuart Mill's classic defense of liberal society, *On Liberty*. Mill argues for liberal policies regarding freedom of expression and lifestyle on the grounds that such policies tend to result in greater average satisfaction than alternative policies.

[6] See Rachels, Ch. 8 for further discussion of such difficulties with utilitarianism; Rachels also provides some indication of how

utilitarians may respond. See Rawls's 1955 paper, "Two Concepts of Rules" (*CP*, 20-46); *TJ*, 144-145; and also the discussion on pages 67-69 of his 1958 paper, "Justice as Fairness" (*CP*, 47-72).

[7] Ronald Dworkin has proposed the idea that rights are essentially "political trumps held by individuals" over considerations of the general good (Dworkin 1977, xi); see especially his essay "Taking Rights Seriously" (Dworkin 1977, 184-205). Jeremy Waldron provides a nice survey of current rights theories, and his bibliography is especially helpful.

[8] The respects in which the case is greatly simplified are many. For example, no account is taken of the dissatisfaction generated by the different distributions. Despite omissions such as this, I think the point will be clear.

[9] Some philosophers have claimed that, with these and related arguments, Rawls won "a decisive victory" over utilitarianism (Feinberg, 116). However, many have defended utilitarianism against Rawls's criticisms, and the issue is by no means settled; see, for example, Sen; Goldman; and Arneson.

[10] In addition to Locke's *Second Treatise* (1689), which is discussed below, the main texts in the contractarian tradition are Hobbes's *Leviathan* (Hobbes 1651), Rousseau's *Of the Social Contract* (Rousseau 1762), and Kant's "Theory and Practice" (in Kant 1970). See Morris, ed. for a collection of accessible critical essays on the contractarianism of Hobbes, Locke, and Rousseau. Hampton provides a helpful survey of the contractarian tradition, as does Kymlicka 1991. For a contemporary expression of contractarianism, see Gauthier 1986.

[11] Locke's *Second Treatise* is divided into nineteen chapters, each of which is further divided into numbered sections. Citations to Locke's *Treatise* will follow the formula: (chapter number.section number); hence II.4 indicates section 4 of Chapter II.

[12] Hence Kant, "But we need by no means to assume that this contract... actually exists as a *fact*, for it cannot possibly be so.... It is in fact merely an *idea* of reason.... For if a law is such that a whole people could not *possibly* agree to it, it is unjust" (Kant, 79).

[13] This characterization is perhaps unduly abstruse. Consider that when someone, upon observing some action of yours, asks you to "imagine if everybody did that," he is proposing a thought experiment.

[14] See *TJ*, 118-123 for a full discussion.

[15] Rawls writes, "The conception of the original position is not intended to explain human conduct except insofar as it tires to account for our moral judgments and helps to explain our having a sense of justice" (*TJ*, 104).

[16] In addition to these social primary goods, Rawls acknowledges a collection of "natural" primary goods such as "health and vigor, intelligence and imagination" (*TJ*, 54).

[17] See Luce and Raiffa for more on the maximin rule.

[18] In *A Theory of Justice*, Rawls warns about taking this analogy too strongly: "The persons in the original position do not, of course, assume that their initial place in society is decided by a malevolent opponent" (*TJ*, 133).

[19] See Sen; Barry, chs. 9 and 10; Hare 1973, 104-107; and R. Wolff, ch. XV. Corrado surveys many of the most pressing concerns. See also Rawls's 1974 essay, "Some Reasons for the Maximin Criterion" (*CP*, 225-231). Philosopher Clark Wolf reports that the maximin argument is "widely regarded as perhaps the single worst argument" in *A Theory of Justice* (Wolf, 104).

[20] To avoid confusion, I have elected to follow several commentators in disposing of Rawls's reference to the "just savings principle" in his formulation of part (a) of the second principle. Barry overlooks this "complication" (Barry, 43) whereas Buchanan omits Rawls's reference to it (Buchanan 1980, 9), as do Mulhall and Swift (Mulhall and Swift, 7).

[21] Rawls claims that these revised formulations meet the criticisms raised in Hart 1973; see *PL*, 5 n.3.

[22] This helpful formulation is found on page 303 of the original edition of *A Theory of Justice* (Cambridge: Harvard University Press, 1971), and curiously has been omitted in the revised edition. However, compare the above statement with *TJ*, 54.

[23] The problem is discussed by Barry; see Barry, 45f.

[24] See Nathanson, Ch. 8 for a similar kind of illustration.

[25] Rawls identifies "unskilled workers" as such a group (*TJ*, 84).

[26] See also T. M. Scanlon's helpful discussion; Scanlon, 192-197.

[27] Critical discussion can be found in Nozick, 213ff.; and Sandel 1998, Ch. 2.

[28] *Political Liberalism* was originally published in 1993. In 1996, a paperback edition was issued containing a new introduction by Rawls and a new final chapter in which Rawls replies to criticisms launched by the philosopher and social theorist, Jurgen Habermas. Citations to *Political Liberalism* will be keyed to the paperback edition.

[29] Sandel's *Liberalism and the Limits of Justice* was originally published in 1982 and was reissued in 1998 with a new Preface and a new closing chapter; citations to this work will be keyed to the Revised Edition of 1998.

[30] Sandel's criticism has come to be associated with a general line of criticism known as the "communitarian critique of liberalism." See also Beiner, Bell, MacIntyre, and Walzer. Mulhall and Swift survey the debate between liberals and communitarians, and Avineri and de-Shalit, eds. contains many of the most important articles.

[31] See also Sandel 1984b.

3

Political Liberalism

A New Framework for Liberal Theory

The criticisms briefly encountered at the close of the preceding chapter have evoked an intriguing response from Rawls in the years since *A Theory of Justice* was first published. Recall that critics and sympathizers found the project of *A Theory of Justice* incomplete; they accordingly sought to excavate and evaluate the tacit "deep theory" presupposed by justice as fairness. Critics such as Michael Sandel have argued that behind Rawls's view lies a problematic theory of the self that can be exposed and refuted.[1] Sympathetic commentators such as Ronald Dworkin and Thomas Nagel contend that a moral theory which grants to all individuals "the abstract right to equal concern and respect" is the "fundamental concept" (Dworkin 1973, 51) underlying the original position; they further maintain that since this fundamental concept can be established by "direct moral arguments" (Nagel 1973, 15), the contractarian devices employed by Rawls are misplaced.

Against the claim that his project is incomplete and in need of further philosophical support, Rawls has advanced a view concerning what one can reasonably expect a liberal political theory to accomplish. Rawls argues that once we are clear about the true nature of liberal political philosophy, we will find that there is no need for a "deep theory" of liberalism and thus that justice as fairness is indeed complete and self-sufficient. Specifically, in *Political Liberalism* Rawls proposes

Political Liberalism
a new "framework" (*PL*, xliii n. 8) of liberal theory and a new way of conceptualizing the methods and objectives of political philosophy. He calls this new style of political theorizing "political liberalism." Rawls's political liberalism is best understood against the background of the older framework he seeks to replace. We begin, then, with the "fundamental" (*PL*, xv) distinction Rawls draws between his own "political" approach to liberal philosophy and what he calls "comprehensive" theories of liberalism.

Comprehensive Liberalism

It can be shown that most traditional liberal political philosophies exhibit a common pattern. Typically, a theorist begins from some basic moral assertion or a view about human nature and then constructs a theory of justice that accommodates this fundamental premise. In this way, traditional liberal theories of justice are "grounded" in or supported by more fundamental philosophical theories. Returning to the beginning of the *Declaration of Independence*, we find that since our Creator has created all persons equal, we enjoy "unalienable" rights to "Life, Liberty, and the pursuit of Happiness" (Jefferson, 601). From this theological view about the source of the moral entitlements of human beings follows all of the major political principles outlined in the *Declaration*. We find a similar strategy employed by John Locke in the document that inspired Jefferson's *Declaration*. In his *Second Treatise*, Locke asserts that men are "all the workmanship of one omnipotent and infinitely wise maker," who created each person to be "equal and independent" (Locke, II.6). The equality and independence which God has bestowed upon all individuals give rise to their natural rights to "life, health, liberty, and possessions" (Locke, II.6). As we saw in the preceding chapter, on Locke's view, the best state is the one that preserves as much of this individual equality and independence as is compatible with an equal degree of equality and independence for all. Thus Locke's liberal political theory rests upon a certain religious view. For one more example, consider the utilitarian theory of liberal justice proposed by John Stuart Mill. On Mill's view, humans are of such a nature as to desire pleasure (and whatever brings pleasure) and to avoid pain (and whatever causes pain). From this basic premise about the nature of human motivation, Mill derives his hedonistic theory of value. Since pleasure is the only thing that is intrinsically good, morally right action consists in maximizing this good; similarly, political justice consists in political institutions, policies, and laws that tend to maximize pleasure across an entire population. Mill's argument in *On Liberty* is that liberal political arrangements are best because they in fact tend to maximize pleasure for the greatest number of persons.

The political theories advanced by Locke, Jefferson, and Mill are good examples of what Rawls calls "comprehensive" theories of liberal justice. They are *comprehensive* liberal theories because they each attempt to establish the justice of liberal political arrangements through an appeal to some more fundamental philosophical theory about human nature or morality. For the comprehensive theorist, then, a theory of justice is not a freestanding philosophical view, but is always in need of the support of what might be called a "background" theory. As we have seen, Mill's theory of political justice is based upon his utilitarianism and hedonism; while Locke's political theory rests upon the claim that God created humans to be equal and independent.

In this way, the comprehensive theorist presents his liberal theory of justice as the application to the political realm of a more general or "comprehensive" philosophical viewpoint, and this comprehensive philosophical view in turn provides the justification for his proposed theory of justice. Hence, if we were to ask Mill why one should endorse a liberal state, he would appeal ultimately to his background theory of utilitarianism.[2] Accordingly, Mill's case for the liberal state is only as strong as his case for utilitarianism; if Mill's background theory fails, so too does his theory of justice. Similarly, Locke's liberalism depends upon his theological background theory; should his theological premise about the nature and origin of human beings fail, so too would his liberal theory.[3]

The aspiration of comprehensive liberalism, then, has been to discover and develop the firmest possible philosophical foundation for liberal politics. The opposing theories of liberal justice found in the history of political philosophy differ mainly in the background theories they presuppose. The traditional presumption has been that there are some basic, undeniable, or, as Jefferson says, "self-evident" (Jefferson, 601) facts about human beings that could serve as the basis for a liberal account of political justice. Traditional comprehensive liberal theories represent different ideas about what these basic facts are and different elaborations of these facts into a liberal political philosophy.

Rawls rejects this traditional way of thinking about the nature and objectives of liberal political theory, and proposes an alternative framework which he calls "political liberalism." According to Rawls, a theory of liberal justice must begin not with some moral or theological claim about human nature, but with the "tradition of democratic thought" (*PL*, 18). A *political* theory of liberal justice thus is not the application to the political realm of some comprehensive philosophical or religious doctrine; a political liberalism is rather an independent and "freestanding" view of justice for the basic structure of society that is neither presented as nor derived from the kind of "deep theory" sought by Dworkin and Nagel (*PL*, 12). Rather than seeking after a philosophical foundation for liberal politics, a political theory of liberal justice attempts to avoid controversial philosophical claims and premises altogether. As Rawls explains in his influential 1985 essay, "Justice as Fairness: Political, not Metaphysical" (*CP*, 388-414), a liberal theory that is *political* as opposed to *comprehensive* "deliberately stays on the surface, philosophically speaking"; it tries to "leave aside philosophical controversies" and "look[s] to avoid philosophy's longstanding problems" (*CP*, 395; cf. *PL*, 10). Accordingly, a political liberalism draws its support not from philosophical theories, but from the tradition of liberalism; it looks not to human nature or to God for its justification, but to "the public culture" of modern liberal democracies and the "shared fund of implicitly recognized basic ideas and principles" this culture supplies (*PL*, 8).

Summing up the concept of a political theory of justice, Rawls explains,

> In saying that a conception of justice is political I . . . mean three things . . . : that it is framed to apply solely to the basic structure of society, its main political, social, and economic institutions as a unified scheme of social cooperation; that it is presented independently of any wider comprehensive religious or philosophical doctrine; and that it is elaborated in terms of fundamental political ideas viewed as implicit in the public culture of a democratic society. (*PL*, 223)

Hence we may say that a *political* liberalism is a theory of justice that "is worked out for a specific kind of subject," namely, the basic structure of a democratic society.[4] That is, a political theory of justice does not attempt to define justice *in general* or with regard to all spheres of life, but is restricted to distributive issues facing a democratic society's main political, social, and economic institutions. Furthermore, a political theory of liberal justice does not derive from and is not cast in terms of any comprehensive philosophical or religious theory. Whereas comprehensive theories such as Mill's utilitarian liberalism try to justify liberal justice in terms of a "background" moral theory, a political theory of justice "tries to elaborate a reasonable conception [of justice] for the basic structure alone and involves, so far as possible, no wider commitment to any other doctrine" (*PL*, 13). Since the political liberal tries to avoid commitment and reference to other philosophical theories, he must restrict himself to the "fundamental ideas seen as implicit in the public political culture of a democratic society" in formulating his conception of justice (*PL*, 13). Rawls insists that this function of organizing the "implicitly shared ideas and principles" (*PL*, 14) of liberal democratic citizens into a coherent conception of justice for the basic structure of society is "the most we can expect" from political philosophy; "nor do we need more" (*CP*, 410).

Justice as Fairness as a Political Liberalism

Whereas in *A Theory of Justice* Rawls presented his view as a comprehensive theory of justice, in *Political Liberalism* justice as fairness is cast as a strictly political liberalism (*PL*, xlii). It is important to mention that in formulating justice as fairness as a strictly political conception, Rawls retains all of the essential features of justice as fairness encountered in the preceding chapter. The original position, the veil of ignorance, and the two principles of justice remain "substantively the same" (*PL*, xvi) as they were in *A Theory of Justice*, and consequently shall not be reviewed in the present chapter. As we have said, what changes, or is clarified,[5] in *Political Liberalism* is the *nature* of Rawls's theory of justice. According to the approach taken in *Political Liberalism*, justice as fairness deliberately avoids "deep" philosophical theories of human nature or the self. As a political liberalism, justice as fairness does not require a background theory; it rather attempts to articulate a coherent conception of justice which accommodates the "considered convictions" of citizens of liberal-democratic societies (*PL*, 8).

Note that if we understand justice as fairness as a political conception of justice, the kinds of criticisms and concerns introduced by Sandel, Dworkin, and Nagel dissolve. These critics presumed that *A Theory of Justice* was proposing a comprehensive theory; they sought after the philosophical premises underlying justice as fairness, and either criticized them, or found Rawls's contractarian arguments inadequate to establish them. However, if justice as fairness is a political conception of liberal justice, then there is no "deeper political theory" (Dworkin 1973, 37) underlying Rawls's view, and no "secret" lurking behind the original position (Sandel 1998, 132). Consequently, there is no basis for Sandel's critique, and no reason to lament the absence of "direct moral arguments" (Nagel 1973, 15) for Rawls's principles of justice.

Nonetheless, Rawls's move to a political conception of justice has seemed to some liberal philosophers a bit too convenient or even *ad hoc*; many have expressed dissatisfaction with Rawls's political liberalism.[6] Typically, a philosopher cannot respond to criticisms of his theory by simply adjusting or redefining the nature of the theory itself; if he does revise or clarify points pertaining to the general aim or scope of his view, he still needs to provide an account of why one should accept his theory. Therefore, even though Rawls cannot appeal to a philosophical theory to support his political conception of justice, he must give *some* reason why we should adopt a theory of justice that "stays on the surface" and avoids philosophical commitment. Why should we accept justice as fairness as a political conception of liberal justice? To put the same question in a different way, Why should we abandon the project of comprehensive liberalism?

Rawls's response to this question is highly complex. His elaboration of the concept of a strictly political liberalism is understandably complicated: political liberalism marks a new approach to political philosophy, it therefore employs a network of novel concepts which need to be carefully explained before the view as a whole can be assessed.

The Political Conception of the Person

Since political liberalism starts "within the tradition of democratic thought" (*PL*, 18), it understands society to be "a fair system of cooperation over time, from one generation to the next" (*PL*, 15). That is, political liberalism draws upon the idea "implicit in the public culture of a democratic society" that the social order is not a "fixed natural order," but the product of the cooperative decisions and actions of the citizens that comprise it (*PL*, 15). Accordingly, political liberalism adopts the "everyday conception" of persons as free and equal agents who have the requisite capacities to be "fully cooperating members of society over a complete life" (*PL*, 18). This view of persons is not to be understood as part of a philosophical theory of human nature or the self. Looking to avoid controversial philosophical premises, political liberalism employs what Rawls calls the "political conception of the person" (*PL*, 29). In liberal democratic societies, citizens conceive of themselves and of each other as being "free and equal" (*PL*, 19). Their freedom and equality derives from certain psychological abilities. More specifically, Rawls contends that persons have two "moral powers," namely, the "capacity for a sense of justice" and "the capacity for a conception of the good" (*PL*, 34). The capacity for a sense of justice is the ability "to understand, to apply, and to act from the public conception of justice which characterizes the fair terms of social cooperation"; the capacity for a conception of the good is the ability "to form, to revise, and rationally pursue a conception of one's rational advantage or good" (*PL*, 19; cf. *PL*, 30).

In virtue of these two powers, citizens of liberal democratic societies try at once to relate to each other on terms which each person can endorse as fair and to advance their own particular visions of the good life. Hence, political liberalism further supposes that individuals "have at any given time a determinate conception of the good that they try to achieve" (*PL*, 19). This conception identifies "what is valuable in human life"; it consists of,

> . . . a more or less determinate scheme of final ends, that is, ends we want to realize for their own sake, as well as attachments to other persons and loyalties to various groups and associations. (*PL*, 19)

Rawls assumes that each citizen affirms some such conception of the good. Usually, this conception of the good is couched within what Rawls calls a "comprehensive doctrine." That is, persons typically derive their understanding of what is valuable or worth pursuing in life from some more general philosophical or religious doctrine.[7] A comprehensive doctrine is a more or less systematic philosophical or religious account of human nature, the relation of humans to the rest of the world, the mark of proper conduct, and the nature of human happiness. A comprehensive doctrine is what is popularly called a "philosophy of life"; one's comprehensive view informs one's life at the deepest level.

The Fact of Reasonable Pluralism

Reasonable Pluralism as a Fact

The cornerstone of political liberalism is the "fact of reasonable pluralism" (*PL* 36).[8] When we look around our democratic society we find that a plurality of distinct and incompatible comprehensive doctrines flourishes among our fellow citizens. Our neighbors, co-workers, classmates, friends, and perhaps even our close relatives pursue different conceptions of the good life, subscribe to different religious views, and strive for different goals. Moreover, we find that many of the persons with whom we disagree about philosophical, moral, and religious essentials are quite intelligent, sincere, well-intentioned, fair-minded, and, in a word, *reasonable*. We find that some persons who hold comprehensive views which differ from our own often have *good reasons* for believing as they do, even though we find these reasons uncompelling. That is, we find that persons who affirm comprehensive doctrines which differ significantly from our own are not *necessarily* foolish or irrational, and that some comprehensive doctrines which differ from our own are reasonable.

Rawls insists that the "diversity of reasonable comprehensive religious, philosophical, and moral doctrines found in modern democratic societies is not a mere historical condition that may soon pass away" (*PL*, 36), but is the "long-run outcome of the work of human reason under enduring free institutions" (*PL*, 129). Accordingly, reasonable pluralism is "not an unfortunate condition of human life," but rather a "permanent feature" of a liberal society (*PL*, 37). Hence the *fact* of reasonable pluralism:

> Under political and social conditions secured by the basic rights and liberties of free institutions, a diversity of conflicting and irreconcilable—and what's more, reasonable—comprehensive doctrines will come about and persist if such diversity does not already obtain. (*PL*, 36)

As Rawls explains it in his 1997 essay, "The Idea of Public Reason Revisited" (*CP*, 573-615),

> . . . a basic feature of democracy is the fact of reasonable pluralism—the fact that a plurality of conflicting reasonable comprehensive doctrines, religious, philosophical, and moral is the normal result of its culture and free institutions. (*CP*, 573)

62

A corollary to the fact of reasonable pluralism is what Rawls calls the "fact of oppression" (*PL*, 37). Since a plurality of reasonable comprehensive doctrines is the "inevitable outcome" of human reason under free institutions, wide-spread social agreement on a single comprehensive doctrine can be achieved only through oppression. Rawls explains,

> . . . a continuing shared understanding on one comprehensive religious, philosophical, or moral doctrine can be maintained only by the oppressive use of state power. If we think of political society as a community united in affirming one and the same comprehensive doctrine, then the oppressive use of state power is necessary for political community. In the society of the Middle Ages, more or less united in affirming the Catholic faith, the Inquisition was not an accident; its suppression of heresy was needed to preserve that shared religious belief. (*PL*, 37; cf. *CP*, 475)

The fact of oppressions is of course not limited to religious comprehensive doctrines. There is no comprehensive doctrine which could serve as the basis for the conception of justice in a free society.[9] Rawls continues,

> The same holds, I believe, for any reasonable comprehensive philosophical and moral doctrine, whether religious or nonreligious. A society united on a reasonable form of utilitarianism, or on the reasonable liberalisms of Kant and Mill, would likewise require the sanctions of state power to remain so. (*PL*, 37)

The Burdens of Judgment

Why should reasonable pluralism be a "permanent feature" (*PL*, 36) of a free society? It may seem that sincere, cooperative, and rational persons should *eventually* be able to come to agreement about the moral, philosophical, and religious questions that divide them. Why is it the case that disagreements persist despite "our conscious attempt to reason with each other" (*PL*, 55)? Why are disagreements over philosophical, moral, and religious doctrines *irresolvable*?

To explain the persistence of conflict over comprehensive views in a free society, Rawls introduces an account of "the many hazards involved in the correct (and conscientious) exercise of our powers of

Political Liberalism

reason and judgment in the ordinary course of political life" (*PL*, 56); Rawls calls these obstacles to agreement the "burdens of judgment" (*PL*, 54).[10] Paraphrasing a cumbersome passage in *Political Liberalism*, philosopher Stephen Mulhall and political scientist Adam Swift explain the burdens of judgment as follows:

> They include such factors as the following: the evidence bearing on the case is complex and conflicting; the weight to be attached to any give piece of evidence is contestable; our concepts are vague and subject to hard cases; and our judgments are imponderably but decisively and differently influenced by the whole course of our individual moral experience.[11] (Mulhall and Swift, 177)

In this way, Rawls explains why pluralism exists in a free society. As everyone is "equally subject to the burdens of judgment" (*PL*, 62), we should expect the "diversity of conflicting and irreconcilable . . . comprehensive doctrines" to persist for as long as we live in a free society (*PL*, 36).

Reasonable Pluralism and Reasonable Persons

We have seen that, on Rawls's view, the fact of reasonable pluralism is a fundamental characteristic of a free society. However, we have not yet specified the significance of the qualifier, "reasonable." The fact of reasonable pluralism is the fact that in a free society a plurality of *reasonable* comprehensive views will flourish among citizens. Accordingly, the fact of reasonable pluralism is to be distinguished from the fact of pluralism as such (*PL*, 36). Free institutions will generate a wide variety of comprehensive views, but not all of these will be reasonable; some persons in a free society will hold "unreasonable, irrational, and even mad" (*PL*, xvii) or "aggressive" (*PL*, 144) comprehensive doctrines. Among the comprehensive doctrines affirmed by citizens in a free society, it is the reasonable ones with which political liberalism is primarily concerned. As for the unreasonable doctrines operative within society, "the problem is to contain them so that they do not undermine the unity and justice of society" (*PL*, xvii).[12]

What then is it for a comprehensive doctrine to be "reasonable"? According to Rawls, a comprehensive doctrine is reasonable if it is compatible with the "essentials of a democratic regime" (*PL*, xvi; cf. *CP*, 574). In particular, reasonable comprehensive doctrines accept the

64

idea that society is a fair system of cooperation over time among free and equal citizens. Therefore, any comprehensive doctrine that opposes liberal democratic forms of society is unreasonable. For example, comprehensive doctrines according to which basic rights and political power ought to be distributed according to race, sex, or ethnicity reject the idea that citizens are equal, and thus are unreasonable. Similarly, comprehensive doctrines which promote the idea that society should be organized according to a particular hierarchical or theocratic scheme deny that society is a fair system of cooperation; they are for this reason also unreasonable.[13]

Rawls applies the qualifier "reasonable" to persons as well. On Rawls's view, a reasonable person is one who holds a reasonable comprehensive doctrine (*PL*, 59). Accordingly, we say that reasonable persons divided at fundamental religious and philosophical levels nevertheless accept the fundamental ideas essential to a democratic society. They hence seek friendly working relations with each other; they "desire for its own sake a social world in which they, as free and equal, can cooperate with others on terms all can accept" (*PL*, 50). Thus reasonable persons do not insist that social and political arrangements reflect or favor their own comprehensive view; a reasonable person recognizes that, due to the burdens of judgment, his fellow reasonable citizens will affirm comprehensive doctrines which differ significantly from his own. Moreover, reasonable persons propose terms of social association and political decision which do not derive exclusively from their own comprehensive doctrine; they accept the fact of reasonable pluralism and try to cooperate with those with whom they disagree over philosophical, moral, and religious essentials; they are ready "to propose fair terms of cooperation it is reasonable to expect others to endorse" (*PL*, 81).

Since they seek fair terms of cooperation, reasonable persons "will think it unreasonable to use political power, should they possess it, to repress comprehensive doctrines that are not unreasonable, though different from their own" (*PL*, 60). As reasonable persons accept the fact of reasonable pluralism, they recognize that, "When there is a plurality of reasonable comprehensive doctrines, it is unreasonable or worse to use the sanctions of state power to correct, or punish those who disagree with us" (*PL*, 138).

Of course, each person believes that his own comprehensive doctrine is true, and that any comprehensive doctrine that is incompatible with his own is false. However, a reasonable person accepts the burdens of judgment and recognizes that it is possible to be reasonable and yet fail to see the truth. Accordingly,

Political Liberalism

It is vital to the idea of political liberalism that we may with perfect consistency hold that it would be unreasonable to use political power to enforce our own comprehensive view, which we must, of course, affirm as either reasonable or true. (*Pl*, 138)

A reasonable person therefore maintains a distinction between his individual or private life, which is governed by his philosophical, moral, or religious comprehensive view, and the "domain of the political," which is governed by a political conception of justice (*PL*, 38).[14] Rawls explains:

For we always assume that citizens have two views, a comprehensive and a political view; and that their overall view can be divided into two parts, suitably related. We hope that by doing this we can in working political practice ground the constitutional essentials and basic institutions of justice solely in those political values, with these values understood as the basis of public reason and justification. (*PL*, 140)

The Idea of an Overlapping Consensus

Reasonable Pluralism and the Question of Stability

Any liberal political theory will presume that in order for a regime to persist over time and be stable, it "must be willingly and freely supported by at least a substantial majority of its politically active citizens" (*PL*, 38). Whereas comprehensive liberal theorists assumed that the stability of a liberal society required widespread agreement among citizens on a single comprehensive view, such as Locke's doctrine of natural rights or Mill's hedonism, the political liberal recognizes the "absolute depth" of the "irreconcilable latent conflict" among reasonable citizens at the level of comprehensive doctrines (*PL*, xxvi). Hence a political liberalism must confront the "question of stability" (*PL*, 140): If a liberal society is to avoid dissolving into a volatile collection of "contending doctrinal confessions and hostile social classes" (*PL*, 36), it must win the support of its citizens; however, assuming that free citizens affirm a plurality of distinct and incompatible philosophical, moral, and religious views, how can they be expected to agree upon and mutually support a common conception

66

of justice? To formulate the question in a general way, Can a society of free persons be stable?

The fact of reasonable pluralism thus opens the question of stability. Rawls insists that "A constitutional regime does not require an agreement on a comprehensive doctrine: the basis of its social unity lies elsewhere" (*PL*, 63). Here we may ask, If the basis of the social unity of a democratic regime does not lie in a shared comprehensive view, where does it reside? Rawls needs to provide an account of the stability of a regime of political liberalism. The concept of an "overlapping consensus" is supposed to do this, and is best understood in contrast with an alternative account of stability which Rawls calls "modus vivendi."

Modus Vivendi versus Overlapping Consensus

It may seem that, given the fact of reasonable pluralism, the best a liberal society can hope for by way of stability is what Rawls calls a "modus vivendi" agreement (*PL*, 145) on a political conception of justice. That is, we may imagine persons holding diverse and incompatible reasonable comprehensive doctrines agreeing to a liberal political arrangement as a matter of concession; such persons would endorse the political conception of justice as a second-best, less than ideal arrangement. When a citizen endorses a liberal conception of justice as a modus vivendi, he accepts the liberal regime as a passable compromise between what he sees as the best political arrangement (i.e., a conception of justice based solely upon his own comprehensive doctrine) and the worst (i.e., a conception of justice based solely upon a comprehensive doctrine that is incompatible with his own).

As an illustration of a liberal political arrangement accepted as a modus vivendi, Rawls considers the situation concerning Catholics and Protestants of the sixteenth century. Rawls explains,

> Both faiths held that it was the duty of the ruler to uphold the true religion and to repress the spread of heresy and false doctrine. In such a case the acceptance of the principle of toleration would indeed be a mere modus vivendi, because if either faith becomes dominant, the principle of toleration would no longer be followed. (PL, 148)

Thus we may imagine a liberal society whose stability is not based upon agreement upon a single comprehensive doctrine, but rather upon a balance of power among the competing doctrines citizens endorse.

Rawls insists, however, that a political conception of justice "must not be political in the wrong way"; that is,

> It must not be political in the sense of merely specifying a workable compromise between known and existing interests, nor political in looking to the particular comprehensive doctrines known to exist in society and in then being tailored to gain their allegiance. (*PL*, 491)

It is clear, then, that a modus vivendi liberalism would be political in the wrong way; the "form and content" of such a liberalism would be contingent upon "the existing balance of political power" among the comprehensive doctrines operative within society (*PL*, 142). Consequently, the stability of society based upon a modus vivendi agreement on its conception of justice is "contingent on circumstances remaining such as not to upset the fortunate convergence of interests" (*PL*, 147). That is, a citizen's commitment to the conception of justice will persist only for as long as his favored comprehensive doctrine is too weak to dominate the others. Should the balance of power be upset and his own view gain ascendancy, he would swiftly abandon the liberal conception of justice.

It may seem that a liberal society based upon a modus vivendi agreement is unacceptable simply because it is unlikely to be long-lasting. However, even if we were to postulate a society in which the relative power among competing comprehensive doctrines was fixed and distributed such that a liberal regime could be long-lasting, Rawls would still be unsatisfied. As philosophers Chandran Kukathas and Philip Pettit explain,

> The stability Rawls is looking for . . . is not the fleeting stability that comes with sound institutional design to moderate the contest for power among competing interests. Stability is a condition in which there is deep-seated agreement on fundamental questions about the basic structure of society. (Kukathas and Pettit 1990, 142)

According to Rawls, stability requires that "people who grow up under just institutions (as the political conception defines them) acquire a normally sufficient sense of justice so that they generally comply with those institutions" (*PL*, 141). Rawls thus insists that if a liberal society is to be stable, its political conception of justice must be endorsed not as a "mere modus vivendi" but by what he calls an "overlapping consensus" (*PL*, 147).

Where a liberal political arrangement is the focus of an overlapping consensus, its political conception of justice is adopted by citizens from *within* their respective comprehensive doctrines; that is, where there is an overlapping consensus, each citizen sees the conception of justice governing the basic structure of society as an appropriate manifestation in the political realm of his own comprehensive doctrine. In this way, Rawls sees a political conception of justice as a "module, an essential constituent part" that "fits into and can be supported by various reasonable comprehensive doctrines that endure in the society regulated by it" (*PL*, 12). Rawls explains,

> An overlapping consensus, therefore, is not merely a consensus on accepting certain authorities, or on complying with certain institutional arrangements, founded on a convergence of self- or group interests. All those who affirm the political conception start from within their own comprehensive view and draw on the religious, philosophical, and moral grounds it provides. (*PL*, 147)

A liberal conception of justice that is the focus of an overlapping consensus is stable not simply because it is likely to be long-lasting, but because it is endorsed by its citizens in a way which gives them reason to uphold its principles regardless of the balance of power among their respective comprehensive doctrines. Thus, where there is an overlapping consensus, citizens endorse the political conception of justice by which they are governed "for its own sake" and "on its own merits," not a second-best compromise (*PL*, 148). Accordingly, citizens "will not withdraw their support of it should the relative strength of their view in society increase and eventually become dominant . . . the political conception will still be supported regardless of shifts in the distribution of political power" (*PL*, 148). Hence, a political conception of liberal justice that is the focus of an overlapping consensus of the reasonable comprehensive doctrines operative within the society it governs will be stable.[15]

Political Justification through Public Reason

We have seen how political liberalism addresses the question of stability. The concept of an overlapping consensus explains how it is possible for a group of reasonable persons profoundly divided on philosophical, moral, and religious fundamentals may nonetheless come to endorse a common political conception of justice to govern the basic structure of their society. The theorist of political liberalism attempts to formulate a conception of justice that can function as a

Political Liberalism

"module" that fits into every reasonable comprehensive doctrine operative within society; in this way, each citizen comes to endorse the political conception of liberal justice from within his own comprehensive doctrine. In *Political Liberalism*, Rawls presents justice as fairness as such a view.

The strategy of looking for social stability in a political conception of justice that is supported by an overlapping consensus of reasonable comprehensive doctrines raises the following concern. Suppose that Rawls's political conception of justice as fairness can indeed be the focus of an overlapping consensus. This means that all reasonable citizens in our society can endorse justice as fairness from within the framework of their own comprehensive doctrines. Accordingly, the utilitarians among us support Rawls's two principles of justice on utilitarian grounds, Catholic citizens see the two principles as the proper expression in the political realm of their own moral commitments, our Buddhist neighbors likewise endorse justice as fairness from within their own philosophical view, and so on. In this way, all reasonable citizens will mutually support justice as fairness, and consequently society will be stable.

However, a democratic society requires more of its citizens than an initial agreement on the conception of justice for the basic structure of society. In a democratic state, citizens share "equally in ultimate political power" (*PL*, xlvi; cf. *PL*, 214): they are called upon to participate in the continuing processes by which laws are made, representatives and officials are elected and appointed, and political actions are decided. When reasonable citizens who have joined the overlapping consensus on Rawls's two principles of justice come together to discuss and decide specific issues of public policy, they may discover the common ground which seemed to unite them and make possible their cooperative deliberations quickly receding.

Since reasonable citizens seek fair terms of social cooperation with their fellow citizens, whom they regard as free and equal, they accept what Rawls calls the "criterion of reciprocity":

> Our exercise of political power is proper only when we sincerely believe that the reasons we offer for our political action may reasonably be accepted by other citizens as a justification of those actions. (*PL*, xlvi)

Hence reasonable citizens conduct their public discussions according to the strictures of what Rawls calls "public reason":

> This means that in discussing constitutional essentials and matters of basic justice we are not to appeal to comprehensive religious and philosophical doctrines—to what we as

70

individuals or members of associations see as the whole truth—nor to elaborate economic theories of general equilibrium, if these are in dispute. As far as possible, the knowledge and ways of reasoning that ground our affirming the principles of justice and their application to constitutional essentials and basic justice are to rest on the plain truths now widely accepted, or available, to citizens generally.[16] (*PL*, 224-225)

When following public reason, citizens exercise what the philosopher Bruce Ackerman has aptly described as "conversational restraint" (Ackerman, 16); that is, they resolve to formulate their arguments for their political choices in terms which stand apart from their own comprehensive doctrines and agree to remove from the agenda of public discussion "the most decisive issues, serious contention about which must undermine the bases of social cooperation" (*PL*, 157).

Of course, the constraints set by the idea of public reason do not apply to all political discussion in all forums. Rawls specifies the questions and situations to which public reason applies. Public reason applies not to all political questions and deliberations, but only to those concerning what Rawls calls "constitutional essentials" and matters of "basic justice"; generally, these are questions concerning "who has the right to vote . . . what religions are to be tolerated . . . who is to be assured fair equality of opportunity, or to hold property" (*PL*, 214).[17] Moreover, public reason does not apply to "personal deliberations" concerning political questions or to political reasoning conducted by "members of associations such as churches and universities"; the limits do apply, however, when citizens "engage in political advocacy in the public forum" and hence when they engage in political campaigns (*PL*, 215). The strictures of public reason also hold when citizens are deliberating about how they should vote "when constitutional essentials and matters of basic justice are at stake"; Rawls notes,

> Thus, the ideal of public reason not only governs the public discourse of elections insofar as the issues involve those of fundamental questions, but also how citizens are to cast their vote on these questions. (*PL*, 215)

The ideal of public reason hence establishes an ideal of citizenship in a democratic regime. Ideal democratic citizens recognize the moral duty of civility (*PL*, 217) which requires that they be able "to explain to one another on those fundamental questions how the principles and policies they advocate and vote for can be supported by the political values of public reason"; they accordingly are ready to "listen to others" (*PL*, 217) and "meet others halfway" (*PL*, 157),

71

exercising "fairmindedness in deciding when accommodations to their views should reasonably be made" (*PL*, 217). In this way, "Understanding how to conduct oneself as a democratic citizen includes understanding an ideal of public reason" (*PL*, 218)

The Necessity of Political Liberalism

With the fundamental concepts of political liberalism in place, we conclude this chapter with a brief discussion of why Rawls thinks liberals must pursue a strictly political conception of justice. Rawls's argument is simple: If we accept the fact of reasonable pluralism, along with the burdens of judgment and the corresponding account of reasonableness, we must reject the project of comprehensive liberalism and adopt a political approach to liberal philosophy. To see this, recall that the objective of the comprehensive theorist is to provide the philosophical foundation of liberal political theory. This foundation was traditionally sought in moral and religious accounts of human nature. However, any such account will constitute or imply a comprehensive doctrine, and one of the basic intuitive ideas "implicit in the public culture of a democratic society" (*PL*, 15) is that disagreement over comprehensive doctrines is the "long-run outcome of the work of human reason under enduring free institutions" (*PL*, 129). So, we may expect that in a free society, persons will hold different and incompatible philosophical, moral, and religious views. Therefore, in a free society, there will be no comprehensive view affirmed by all citizens.[18]

If we believe that society is a fair system of cooperation among free and equal persons, we cannot endorse a political arrangement which requires agreement on a single comprehensive doctrine. Such an arrangement would necessarily involve oppression, and a state which oppresses its citizens does not treat them as free and equal persons. Hence we may conclude that the very idea of a comprehensive theory serving as the basis of the conception of justice for a liberal society is incoherent; society-wide agreement on a single comprehensive doctrine can be achieved only through oppression, and oppression is inconsistent with liberalism. Therefore, the aspiration of the comprehensive theorist of liberal justice is misguided. As Rawls puts it,

> ... the question the dominant tradition has tried to answer has no answer: no comprehensive doctrine is appropriate as a political conception for a constitutional regime. (*PL*, 135)

Political Liberalism

According to Rawls, a consistent liberalism must be *thoroughly* liberal; that is, it must be liberal not only in its conception of justice, but also in its *justification* for its conception of justice. Rawls explains, "Political liberalism applies the principle of toleration to philosophy itself" (*PL*, 10); like a liberal society, a liberal theory must tolerate the plurality of incompatible but reasonable comprehensive views. Therefore, a consistent theory of liberal justice must be a *political* conception of liberal justice; it must not be cast in terms of any particular comprehensive doctrine, but must appeal only to the most general and widely shared ideas "implicitly recognized" in the "public culture" of liberal democratic societies. To philosophical questions regarding human nature, religion, and morality, a political liberalism "does not speak" (*PL*, 127). Indeed, in order to "stay on the surface" of philosophical controversy, a political liberalism attempts to abstain from referring to its own conception of justice and the judgments which follow from it as "true." Rawls reminds us, "Which moral judgments are true, all things considered, is not a matter for political liberalism" (*PL*, xx).[19]

The aim of a political liberalism, then, is not that of uncovering the philosophical foundations of a liberal conception of justice; it is rather that of formulating a liberal conception of justice in strictly political terms which can be the focus of an overlapping consensus among the reasonable comprehensive doctrines operative within society. Rawls's main contention in *Political Liberalism*, then, is that his conception of liberal justice, justice as fairness, is the most reasonable conception of liberal justice for a society of free and equal persons.

Endnotes

[1] A similar line of criticism is pursued in Bell; MacIntyre; and Taylor 1985a.

[2] Mill writes, "I regard utility as the ultimate appeal on all ethical questions" (Mill, 15).

[3] Note that Locke advises liberal society to not tolerate atheists. In his *Letter Concerning Toleration*, Locke writes, "those are not at all to be tolerated who deny the being of a God . . . . The taking away of God, though but even in thought, dissolves all" (Locke 1689b, 313). On this also see Gauthier, 1977.

[4] For more on this, see Rawls's "The Basic Structure as Subject" (*PL*, Lecture VII).

[5] Rawls sometimes writes as if his later work merely clarifies justice as fairness, which, due to some unfortunate ambiguities of expression in *A Theory of Justice*, has been misunderstood (*PL*, xvii). At other times, Rawls uses the stronger language of "reformulation," "transformation," and "adjustment" to characterize his later work (*PL*, xliii; xiv).

[6] See, for example, R. Dworkin 1988; Hampton 1989; Scheffler; and the essays collected in Davion and Wolf, eds. See Cohen 1993; Gutmann 1985 and Rorty 1988 for sympathetic reactions to Rawls's turn.

[7] The concept of a "comprehensive doctrine" has already been alluded to in our discussion of comprehensive liberalism; a comprehensive theory of liberal justice is one which is based upon a comprehensive doctrine.

[8] Rawls writes, "It is the fact of reasonable pluralism that leads— at least to me—to the idea a political conception of justice and so to the idea of political liberalism" (*PL*, xlvii).

[9] It is interesting to contrast Aristotle: "For it is a peculiarity of humans . . . to have perception of good and bad, just and unjust, and the like; and community in these things makes a household and a city" (Aristotle 1996, 1253a15).

[10] Cf. "The Domain of the Political and Overlapping Consensus," where they are characterized as the "burdens of reason" (*CP*, 475-478).

[11] See *PL*, 56-57 for the passage of which this is a paraphrase; cf. *CP*, 476-477.

[12] Rawls's views on how a liberal society should deal with citizens who affirm unreasonable comprehensive doctrines are intriguing and controversial, but beyond the scope of the present study. See Friedman and the final chapter of Sandel 1998 for the standard concerns, which are quite serious.

[13] Note that according to these criteria, the political view of Aristotle is unreasonable.

[14] This way of detaching politics from any broader concern with the good life is characterized by Ronald Dworkin as the "strategy of discontinuity"; for Dworkin's criticisms, see Dworkin 1988. According to Dworkin, liberal politics does not occupy a special domain apart from philosophical, moral, and religious doctrines, but is rather "continuous with the best personal ethics and with the right philosophical view of the good life" (Dworkin 1988, 193).

[15] For criticism of Rawls on these points, see Mills; Dauenhauer; Hershovitz; and Scheffler.

[16] Rawls characterizes public reason as the reason of the supreme court (*PL*, 231); thus "To check whether we are following public reason we might ask: how would our argument strike us presented in the form of a supreme court opinion? Reasonable? Outrageous?" (*PL*, 254).

[17] See *PL*, 227-230 for a complete discussion of "constitutional essentials" and "basic justice."

[18] Conversely, a society in which all citizens hold the same comprehensive doctrine is oppressive and thus not free (*PL*, 37).

[19] On this, see Nagel 1987; Raz 1990; and Estlund.

4

Epilogue:
Rawls's Achievement

Thomas Nagel dedicated his 1991 book in political philosophy, *Equality and Partiality*, to "John Rawls, who changed the subject." Having surveyed the main contours of Rawls's thought, we are able to see that Nagel's dedication deliberately trades on an ambiguity: there are several senses in which John Rawls "changed the subject" of political philosophy.

Rawls's *A Theory of Justice* launched an innovative and fascinating theory of liberal justice whose influence is present today in all areas of moral and political thought. This influence is due in part to the fact that *A Theory of Justice* is a model work of philosophical argumentation. In *A Theory of* Justice, Rawls not only does the critical work of advancing creative and plausible arguments against the leading accounts of justice of our day, he also constructs and deploys a series of imaginative considerations in favor of his own theory. This combination of rigorous criticism and argumentation with creativity and insight set a new standard in political philosophy; in this sense, Rawls changed the subject.

But this alone does not constitute Rawls's achievement, and it does not explain Rawls's impact. In addition, and perhaps more importantly, *A Theory of Justice* exhibits a kind of intellectual ambition that had been missing from political theory for decades. Prior to Rawls, much of our political theorizing was conducted within neatly compartmentalized academic categories; sociologists wrote for other sociologists, economists were read by economists, and political philosophers addressed their ideas only to other philosophers. In many respects, *A Theory of Justice* changed this. Within its pages, Rawls comments on and draws from the work of economists, decision theorists, social scientists, and legal scholars. In Rawls's work, political thinking across many disciplines reached its culmination; Rawls presented a vision of society that took account of all the major findings of the relevant areas of social inquiry, expressed in language accessible to all within the academy and even to many of those outside it. Hence *A Theory of Justice* also marked a return to a conception of the philosophical enterprise according to which philosophy is primarily a synthesizing discipline; on this view, it is the job characteristic of the philosopher to master all the other disciplines, and to articulate a systematic intellectual vision of the world. By proposing an interdisciplinary philosophical vision of political justice, Rawls changed the subject

Moreover, *A Theory of Justice* represented to many the return of systematic, grand-scale political philosophy. Throughout much of the twentieth century, philosophers had taken their discipline to be a separate enterprise with its own problems and methods. In staking out its distinctive turf, philosophy had for the most part given up on moral and political theory, areas of inquiry that to many philosophers looked too much like the social sciences (Ayer, Ch. VI). Insisting that questions of morality and political justice could not be settled rationally, many philosophers turned to the chores of linguistic analysis; consequently moral and political philosophy was in a nearly moribund state for much of the latter part of the century. What *A Theory of Justice* showed is that there is in fact a distinctively philosophical and rational way of examining questions of social justice. By effecting this revival of substantive moral and political philosophy, Rawls changed the subject.

Rawls's work following *A Theory of Justice*, culminating in his *Political Liberalism*, marks yet another sense in which he changed the subject. In *Political Liberalism* Rawls makes a convincing case for rejecting the project of liberal political philosophy as traditionally construed. As we have seen, liberal philosophers have often taken their mission to be that of uncovering the philosophical foundations of liberal democracy; they have attempted to show that our basic rights to freedom and equality follow from some more fundamental philosophical thesis about human nature, or morality, or God. By insisting that liberal political philosophy begin not with philosophical theories of human nature or moral obligation or God's creation, but with the plain facts about liberal society, and, in particular, the fact of reasonable pluralism, Rawls liberated political philosophers from the task of carrying on intractable debates about philosophical essentials. According to Rawls, liberal political philosophers must focus their efforts on the practical matter of formulating a political conception of justice for reasonable democratic citizens. Freed from their traditional task of searching for philosophical foundations, political philosophers have been able to address matters of political concern to the general public, they have thereby begun to rehabilitate the standing and significance of political and moral philosophy in our popular culture. In short, *Political Liberalism* transformed the very nature of the questions which political philosophers address and the methods they employ when addressing them; this is, in my view, the most important sense in which Rawls changed the subject of liberal philosophy.

Works Cited

Ackerman, Bruce. 1989. "Why Dialogue?" *Journal of Philosophy* LXXXVI, no. 1: 5-24.

Alejandro, Robert. 1997. *The Limits of Rawlsian Justice.* Maryland: Johns Hopkins University Press.

Aristotle. 1962. *Nicomachean Ethics.* Martin Ostwald, translator. New Jersey: Prentice Hall.

_____. 1997. *Politics.* Peter Simpson, translator. Chapel Hill: University of North Carolina Press.

Arneson, Richard J. 2000. "Rawls Versus Utilitarianism in Light of *Political Liberalism.*" In Davion and Wolf, eds.

Avineri, S. and A. De-Shalit, eds. 1992. *Communitarianism and Individualism.* New York: Oxford University Press.

Ayer, A. J. 1936. *Language, Truth, and Logic.* London: Camelot Press.

Baier, Annette. 1987. "The Need for More than Justice." In Marsha Hanen and Kai Nielsen, eds. *Science, Morality and Feminist Theory* (Calgary: University of Calgary Press, 1987).

Barber, Benjamin. 1975. "Justifying Justice: Problems of Psychology, Politics, and Measurement in Rawls." In Daniels, ed.

_____. 1984. *Strong Democracy.* California: University of California Press.

Barry, Brian. 1973. *The Liberal Theory of Justice.* Oxford: Clarendon Press.

Beiner, Ronald. 1992. *What's the Matter With Liberalism?* Berkeley: University of California Press.

Bell, Daniel A. 1993. *Communitarianism and its Critics.* New York: Oxford University Press.

Bentham, Jeremy. 1789. *An Introduction to the Principles of Morals and Legislation.* In Cahn, ed.

Berlin, Isaiah. 1958. "Two Concepts of Liberty." In Berlin, *Four Essays on Liberty* (New York: Oxford University Press, 1969).

Blocker, H. Gene and Elizabeth H. Smith, eds. 1980. *John Rawls' Theory of Social Justice: An Introduction.* Athens: Ohio University Press.

Brennan, Samantha and Robert Noggle. 2000. "Rawls's Neglected Childhood." In Davion and Wolf, eds.

Buchanan, Allen. 1980. "A Critical Introduction to Rawls' Theory of Justice." In Blocker and Smith, eds.

_____. 1989. "Assessing the Communitarian Critique of Liberalism." Ethics 99: 852-882.

Cahn, Steven and Joram Haber, eds. 1995. *20th Century Ethical Theory.* New Jersey: Prentice Hall.

Cahn, Steven, ed. 1997. *Classics of Political Theory.* New York: Oxford University Press.

Cohen, Joshua. 1993. "Moral Pluralism and Political Consensus." In David Copp, Jean Hampton, and John Roemer, eds. *The Idea of Democracy* (Cambridge: Cambridge University Press, 1993).

Corrado, Gail. 1980. "Rawls, Games, and Economic Theory." In Blocker and Smith, eds.

Crisp, Roger and Dale Jamieson. 2000. "Egalitarianism and a Global Resources Tax: Pogge on Rawls." In Davion and Wolf.

Daniels, Norman, ed. 1989. *Reading Rawls: Critical Studies on Rawls' A Theory of Justice.* California: Stanford University Press.

_____. 1996. *Justice and Justification.* New York: Cambridge University Press.

Dauenhauer, Bernard P. 2000. "A Good Word for a Modus Vivendi." In Davion and Wolf, eds.

Davion, Victoria and Clark Wolf, eds. 2000. *The Idea of a Political Liberalism: Essays on Rawls.* Maryland: Rowman and Littlefield.

Dworkin, Ronald. 1973. "The Original Position." In Daniels, ed.

_____. 1977. *Taking Rights Seriously.* Cambridge: Harvard University Press.

_____. 1978. "Liberalism." In Dworkin, *A Matter of Principle* (Cambridge: Harvard University Press, 1985).

_____. 1988. "Foundations of Liberal Equality." In Stephen Darwall, ed. *Equal Freedom* (Ann Arbor: University of Michigan Press, 1995).

_____. 1993. "Liberty and Pornography." In Dwyer, ed.

Dwyer, Susan, ed. 1995. *The Problem of Pornography*. California: Wadsworth Publishing.

Estlund, David. 1998. "The Insularity of the Reasonable: Why Political Liberalism Must Admit the Truth." *Ethics* 108: 252-275.

Etzioni, Amitai. 1993. *The Spirit of Community*. New York: Simon and Schuster.

Feinberg, Joel. 1975. "Rawls and Intuitionism." In Daniels, ed.

Friedman, Marilyn. 2000. "Rawls on the Political Coercion of Unreasonable People." In Davion and Wolf, eds.

Frohlich, Norman and Joe Oppenheimer. 1992. *Choosing Justice*. California: University of California Press.

Gauthier, David. 1977. "Why Ought One Obey God? Reflections on Hobbes and Locke." In Morris, ed.

_____. 1986. *Morals by Agreement*. Oxford: Oxford University Press.

George, Robert, and Christopher Wolfe, eds. 2000. *Natural Law and Public Reason*. Washington D.C.: Georgetown University Press.

Goldman, Holly Smith. 1980. "Rawls and Utilitarianism." In Blocker and Smith, eds.

Goodin, Robert E. and Philip Pettit, eds. 1993. *A Companion to Contemporary Political Philosophy*. Oxford: Blackwell.

Gutmann, Amy, 1985. "Communitarian Critics of Liberalism." In Avineri and de-Shalit, eds.

Hampton, Jean. 1989. "Should Political Philosophy be Done Without Metaphysics?" *Ethics* 99:791-814.

_____. 1993. "Contract and Consent." In Goodin and Pettit, eds.

Hare, R. M. 1973. "Rawls' Theory of Justice." Reprinted in Daniels, ed.

_____. 1981. *Moral Thinking*. New York: Oxford University Press.

Held, Virginia. 1993. *Feminist Morality*. Chicago: University of Chicago Press.

Held, Virginia, ed. 1995. *Justice and Care*. Colorado: Westview Press.

Hershovitz, Scott. 2000. "A Mere Modus Vivendi?" In Davion and Wolf, eds.

Hobbes, Thomas. 1651. *Leviathan*. In Cahn, ed.

Hume, David. 1748. "Of the Original Contract." In Cahn, ed.

Jefferson, Thomas. 1776. *The Declaration of Independence*. In Cahn, ed.

Kant, Immanuel. 1970. *Political Writings*. Edited by Hans Reiss. Cambridge: Cambridge University Press.

Kekes, John. 1997. *Against Liberalism*. Ithaca: Cornell University Press.

Kukathas, Chandran and Philip Pettit. 1990. *Rawls:* A Theory of Justice *and its Critics.* California: Stanford University Press.

Kymlicka, Will. 1989. *Liberalism, Community, and Culture.* Oxford: Clarendon Press.

_____. 1991. "The Social Contract Tradition." In Peter Singer, ed. *A Companion to Ethics* (Oxford: Blackwell).

Langton, Rae. 1990. "Whose Right? Ronald Dworkin, Women, and Pornographers." In Dwyer, ed.

Locke, John. 1689a. *Second Treatise of Government.* In Cahn, ed.

_____. 1689b. *A Letter Concerning Toleration.* In Cahn, ed.

Luce, R. Duncan and Howard Raiffa. 1957. *Games and Decisions.* New York: John Wiley and Sons.

Lyons, David. 1975. "Nature and Soundness of the Contract and Coherence Arguments." In Daniels, ed.

MacIntyre, Alasdair. 1981. *After Virtue.* Indiana: University of Notre Dame Press.

MacKinnon, Catherine. 1987. "Francis Biddle's Sister: Pornography, Civil Rights, and Speech." In Dwyer, ed.

Michelman, Frank. 1975. "Constitutional Welfare Rights and *A Theory of Justice.*" In Daniels, ed.

Mill, John Stuart. 1991. *On Liberty and Other Essays.* New York: Oxford University Press.

Miller, Richard. 1975. "Rawls and Marxism." In Daniels, ed.

Miller, Fred, Jr. 1995. *Nature, Justice and Rights in Aristotle's* Politics. Oxford: Clarendon Press.

Mills, Claudia. 2000. "Not a Mere Modus Vivendi: The Bases for Allegiance to the Just State." In Davion and Wolf, eds.

Morris, Christopher W., ed. 1999. *The Social Contract Theorists.* Maryland: Rowman and Littlefield.

Mulhall, Stephen and Adam Swift. 1996. *Liberals and Communitarians.* Second Edition. Oxford: Blackwell.

Nagel, Thomas. 1973. "Rawls on Justice." In Daniels, ed.

_____. 1987. "Moral Conflict and Political Legitimacy." *Philosophy and Public Affairs* 16: 215-240.

_____. 1991. *Equality and Partiality.* New York: Oxford University Press.

_____. 1999. "Justice, Justice, Shalt Thou Pursue: The Rigorous Compassion of John Rawls." *The New Republic* 221, No. 17 (25 October 1999):36-41.

Nathanson, Stephen. 1998. *Economic Justice.* New Jersey: Prentice Hall.

Nozick, Robert. 1974. *Anarchy, State, and Utopia*. New York: Basic Books.

Nussbaum, Martha. 1997. *Sex and Social Justice*. New York: Oxford University Press.

Pettit, Philip. 1997. *Republicanism*. New York: Oxford University Press.

Pogge, Thomas. 1989. *Realizing Rawls*. New York: Cornell University Press.

Pyke, Steve. 1995. *Philosophers*. New York: Distributed Art Publishers.

Quinn, Philip. 1995. "Political Liberalisms and their Exclusions of the Religious." *Proceedings and Addresses of the American Philosophical Association* 69, no. 2: 35-56.

Rachels, James. 1999. *The Elements of Moral Philosophy*. Third Edition. Boston: McGraw Hill.

Raz, Joseph. 1986. *The Morality of Freedom*. Oxford: Clarendon Press.
_____. 1990. "Facing Diversity: The Case for Epistemic Abstinence." In Raz, *Ethics in the Public Domain* (New York: Oxford University Press, 1994.)

Rorty, Richard. 1988. "The Priority of Democracy to Philosophy." In Rorty, *Objectivity, Relativism, and Truth* (Cambridge: Cambridge University Press, 1991).

Rousseau, Jean-Jacques. 1762. *Of the Social Contract*. In Cahn, ed.

Ryan, Alan. 1993. "Liberalism." In Goodin and Pettit, eds.

Sandel, Michael. 1984a. "Introduction." In Sandel, ed. *Liberalism and its Critics* (New York: New York University Press, 1984.)
_____. 1984b. "The Procedural Republic and the Unencumbered Self." In Avineri and de-Shalit, eds.
_____. 1996. *Democracy's Discontent*. Cambridge: Harvard University Press.
_____. 1998. *Liberalism and the Limits of Justice*. Second Edition. Cambridge: Cambridge University Press.

Sen, A. K. 1974. "Rawls Versus Bentham: An Axiomatic Examination of the Pure Distrib   on Problem." In Daniels, ed.

Scanlon, T. M. 1975. "Rawls' Theory of Justice." In Daniels, ed.

Scheffler, Samuel. 1994. "The Appeal of Political Liberalism." *Ethics* 105:4-22.

Shaw, William H. 1999. *Contemporary Ethics: Taking Account of Utilitarianism*. Oxford: Blackwell.

Sher, George. 1997. *Beyond Neutrality*. Cambridge: Cambridge University Press.

Sidgwick, Henry. 1874. *Methods of Ethics*. London: Macmillian.

Simpson, Peter. 1990. "Making the Citizens Good: Aristotle's City and its Contemporary Relevance." *Philosophical Forum* XXII, no. 2:149-166.

Smart, J. J. C. 1963. "An Outline of a System of Utilitarian Ethics." In *Utilitarianism: For and Against* (Cambridge: Cambridge University Press, 1963).

Taylor, Charles. 1985a. "Atomism." In Taylor, *Philosophical Papers II*. Cambridge: Cambridge University Press.

_____. 1985b. "What's Wrong with Negative Liberty?" In Taylor, *Philosophical Papers II*. Cambridge: Cambridge University Press.

U. S. President. "Remarks on Presenting the Arts and Humanities Awards." *Weekly Compilation of Presidential Documents* 35, No. 39 (4 October 1999):1821-1886.

Waldron, Jeremy. 1993. "Rights." In Goodin and Pettit, eds.

Walzer, Michael. 1983. *Spheres of Justice*. New York: Basic Books.

Wenar, Leif. 1995. "*Political Liberalism*: An Internal Critique." *Ethics* 106: 32-62.

Wolf, Clark. 2000. "Fundamental Rights, Reasonable Pluralism, and the Moral Commitments of Liberalism." In Davion and Wolf, eds.

Wolff, Jonathan. 1998. "John Rawls: Liberal Democracy Restated." In April Carter and Geoffrey Stokes, eds. *Liberal Democracy and its Critics* (Cambridge: Polity Press, 1998).

Wolff, Robert Paul. 1977. *Understanding Rawls*. New Jersey: Princeton University Press.